Randolph S. Churchill

Twenty-One Years

Weidenfeld and Nicolson

20 New Bond Street London W1

Printed in Great Britain
by C. Tinling and Company Ltd
London, Liverpool and Prescot

CONTENTS

ILLUSTRATIONS

Illustrations

Most of the photographs used in this book are family ones from my own albums. I am indebted to Baroness Asquith of Yarnbury for no 5, to Mr F. J. Wymer and the Camera Press for no 4, to Mr Edwin Smith for no 15 and Mr John Bulmer for no 24.

PART I: 1911–24

I was born in London on 28 May 1911 at 33 Eccleston Square, of poor but honest parents. Born within sound of Bow Bells I was a cockney and, until I was forty, was destined to spend more than half my life in London.

The only surviving salutation that I have been able to find on the occasion of my birth came the very next day. It was from Mr Austen Chamberlain to my father. It is of interest since it shows that during a period of fierce Party conflict there was friendship across the floor of the House.

Austen Chamberlain to WSC
29 May 1911   House of Commons
    Hearty congratulations. I hope all goes well with Mother and boy –
    It is a pity you cannot yet draw the Maternity Benefit[1] but I understand that you are making it up through Government postage.[2]

AUSTEN

I have no recollections of Eccleston Square where my father and mother had lived since their marriage in 1908. When I was born my father was Home Secretary in Mr Asquith's famous Liberal administration, and when I was only a few months old my father became First Lord of the Admiralty and we all moved to Admiralty House overlooking the Horse Guards Parade. We all: that is my father and mother and sister Diana, who was nearly two years older than myself.

Diana and I were very naughty children. I remember throw-

[1] On 4 May 1911 Lloyd George proposed in the House of Commons a maternity benefit of thirty shillings a week. This was incorporated in the National Insurance Bill.

[2] Chamberlain was assuming, rightly or wrongly, that Churchill was using free postage to acknowledge the numerous felicitations he received at this time.

11

ing the nursery maid's wristwatch out of the window from a great height and it shattered on the ground. In the winter Diana and I had white furry rabbit-skin coats. One day we were taken out to tea with some other children, and for some reason we were not accompanied by our own nanny or nursery maid. When we were brought back to Admiralty House by the people with whom we had been having tea, we rolled in our white coats on the steps. When reproved, we said 'We always do that when nanny is not there'. We must have been horrible children. Very few nannies or nursery maids stayed very long. The departures of those we disliked most were serenaded by bumping their bags down the stairs shrilly crying 'Nanny's going, Nanny's going. Hurrah! Hurrah!' Diana was more docile than I was: I could never brook authority or discipline.

The grandeur of Admiralty House and this talk of nannies and nursery maids may seem to belie that my parents were 'poor'. Of course this is a relative term, but since he was twenty-one my father never had any money except what he had earned by his writing and lectures, and most of this must have been expended by the time he married my mother, Miss Clementine Hozier. She came of a famous Scottish family (she was a granddaughter of the seventh Earl of Airlie) but she was as impecunious as my father. She was the beauty of the generation, but she brought no dowry with her.

My father, it is true, had a salary of £3,500 a year as President of the Board of Trade, but, as I was to hear later, politics is a precarious trade and the emoluments of office are far from permanent. Living in the grand world of fashion and politics I suppose that though Income Tax was only one and three pence in the pound (in spite of all that my father's friend Mr Lloyd George could do), my father and mother had often to contrive to make things do; they cannot have managed to save very much during the four years we lived at Admiralty House.

For some reason or other I was not christened for five months. Then the ceremony took place in the crypt of the House of Commons. I was named Randolph Frederick Edward Spencer Churchill; Randolph after my grandfather whom I never knew (he died sixteen years before my birth); Frederick after my father's greatest friend, my godfather, Mr F. E. Smith (later first Earl of Birkenhead); Edward after another godfather, my father's colleague Sir Edward Grey who was Foreign Secretary. Spencer was, of course, a family name, and my true surname was Spencer-Churchill. My father's branch of the family had, however, at some time stopped the use of the hyphen, though it was still preserved in the Court circular whenever Sir Winston had audience of the Sovereign. My godmother was Lady Ridley, a daughter of the first Baron Wimborne and a first cousin of my father's.

I have a shadowy recollection of Sir Edward Grey. I seem to recall when I was ten or eleven a visit he paid, then almost blind, to Chartwell. My godmother I do not remember at all though she died only in 1947 and always sent me nice presents at Christmas. The famous F.E. I got to know quite well, but of him later.

All my three godparents gave me fine silver to mark the occasion of my christening, all of which I preserve and use today. The best was that of Rosie Ridley, a silver tankard dated 1780 from which I still drink my beer and champagne; F.E.'s was a handsome copy of an Elizabethan rose bowl; and Sir Edward Grey's was a modest, but pretty, silver porringer.

I have long marvelled at the fantastically retentive memory of Sir Osbert Sitwell. He is capable of filling volumes with his childhood memories. My memories of my childhood are sparse; and even now when I am trying to relive the period of which I write, nothing extra do I seem able to evoke apart from the memories I have always had.

I remember looking out of a window at Admiralty House and seeing a large muster of soldiers on the Horse Guards

Parade. I asked where they were going and was told: 'The Dardanelles.' This must have been in 1915 when I was four. I didn't know where the Dardanelles were or what the war was all about, but the Dardanelles hung like a storm cloud over Admiralty House and I used to end my nightly prayers: 'God bless Mummy and Papa. God bless the Dardanelles and make me a good boy. Amen.'

I also used to pray for a Mr Jones at this time. I was taken, I suppose by my father, to the House of Commons. Amongst other sights I was shown the pegs on which Members hung their hats. Pointing to the first peg I saw I enquired irrelevantly who hung his hat there. I was told Mr Jones. He rated almost as highly in my prayers as the Dardanelles.

While we were still at Admiralty House my second sister, Sarah, was born. This was the night Antwerp fell. I was three and a half. I don't remember the fall of Antwerp or Sarah's birth. I only heard about these two events later. Before we left Admiralty House in the summer of 1915, a curtain rod fell on Sarah's nose and made a bump on it. I don't remember this either. I have been told about it since. The bump was later removed.

One other thing I remember at Admiralty House. Diana and I used to be taken for a daily morning airing in the Green Park in a double pram. This must have been just before the war. There were people called suffragettes who wanted to get votes for women, which, I later discovered, was a proposal to which my father and Mr Asquith were strongly opposed; so the suffragettes tried to kidnap me in the park. I have a fugitive memory of being pulled out of the pram and of the nursery maid catching hold of me and pulling me back. More strongly etched in my memory is the detective who thereafter discreetly accompanied us on our morning airings lest this half-hearted attempt should be repeated.

I think I remember the coming of the war in August 1914. We were staying at the seaside, I think at a place called 'Hoe

Farm'. There was a lot of excitement and my father had to go to London. One day we were told that war had come. We looked out to sea expecting that German ships would soon come into view but nothing happened, except that my father could not come down from London. We children were all disappointed – no Germans and no Papa.

In May 1915, when we were turned out of Admiralty House, we all went to live at 41 Cromwell Road. We doubled up with my Uncle Jack, my father's younger brother, and my Aunt Goonie and their two children, Johnny who was two years older than me and Peregrine who had just been born. The house was almost opposite the Natural History Museum. On wet afternoons Diana, Johnny and I would be taken there. We did not spend much time looking at the exhibits. We preferred to run along its corridors playing hide and seek and, since hardly anybody seemed interested in the specimens which had been collected in this fine building, we seldom got into any trouble.

While we were at Cromwell Road there were Zeppelin raids on London. These were tremendously exciting since we children would be woken up in the middle of the night, wrapped up in blankets and carried down to the basement where there would be a lot of grown-ups having supper and drinking champagne. We liked Zeppelins very much indeed and thought it a great treat to mix with grown-ups in the middle of the night.

Another memory of mine of Cromwell Road is of one of my father's birthdays. We children had our luncheon upstairs and were always brought down to see the grown-ups finishing their lunch. One day, when it was my father's birthday (30 November, St Andrew's Day), we came down and for some reason or other the grown-ups had only just started eating. My mother had arranged a treat for my father – oysters. When we children came in there was only one left. My father said 'Would you like to try one?' I naturally said 'Yes'. The oyster was put into my mouth. I was horrified and went and spat it into the fire.

I suppose this was in 1917 with food rationing so very strict. Everyone was aghast at my sacrilegious act. I am glad to record that this episode left no permanent psychological or gastronomical scar on my palate, for I have eaten scores of dozens of oysters in later years, with the greatest conceivable delectation.

A little time after we settled down with Uncle Jack and Aunt Goonie in the Cromwell Road, my father went off to the war. I don't remember his departure at all; but I have preserved a letter he wrote me from the trenches:

My dearest Randolph

I am living here in a little farm. It is not so pretty as Hoe Farm, and there are no nice flowers and no pond or trees to play gorilla[1] but there are three large fat dirty pigs. Like the ones we saw in the wood.

The Germans are a long way off and cannot shoot at us here. It is too far. So we are quite safe as long as we stay here. But we can hear the cannons booming in the distance and at night when it is all dark we can see their flashes twinkling in the sky. Soon we are going to go close up to the Germans and then we shall shoot back at them and try to kill them. This is because they have done wrong and caused all this war and sorrow.

Give my very best love to Diana and kiss Sarah for me. Write me a letter yourself soon and I will send you an answer back.

Your ever loving father,

WINSTON S. C.

A little later, I suppose at the end of 1916 or at the beginning of 1917, my father bought a little place in the country, Lullenden near East Grinstead, I imagine with the object of getting us children away from the air raids. We were very happy there and used to go to school at a place called Dormansland in a pony trap. I think we only went there in the morning. The lessons ended with a short religious service and the final hymn was always: 'O God our help in ages past.' Then we used to drive back to Lullenden in the pony trap for luncheon.

It was at this time that I first discovered in a rather macabre way that my father was different from other fathers and was a

[1] Gorilla was the game we used to play in the country. My father would chase us all up the trees and come climbing up after us.

16

Christening photograph: RSC with his mother, 26 October 1911

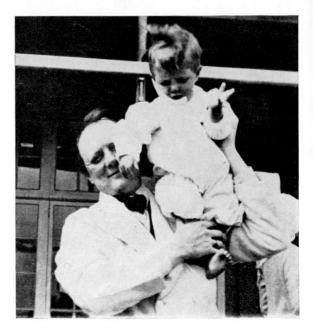

RSC with WSC: summer 1912

Diana Churchill walking in Whitehall with her nurse.
In the perambulator is RSC

great man. I was about five years old at the time and I said to a little boy at school (it makes me blush to recall the episode), 'Will you be my chum?' He said, 'No'. I said 'Why not?' He said, 'Your father murdered my father'. I said: 'What do you mean?' He said, 'At the Dardanelles'. So when I got home I told this to my mother who was naturally distressed at what had happened and explained to me about the Dardanelles. I am sorry to say it made me feel immensely proud for I realised my father was a boss man who could order other fathers about.

My discovery that my father had exceptional powers was reinforced in a more mundane matter. Often my mother and father were not at Lullenden for many weeks. He was making munitions and she was running a lot of canteens for munition workers. One day we heard that my father was coming down that afternoon at tea time. We had run out of jam. My father has never had tea as a meal in his life. He had always said, 'I don't believe in eating between meals'. However, we thought that perhaps he would come and sit with us children while we had our tea. So with a precocious sense of propaganda I collected ten or twelve empty jam pots and put them on the tea table. My father is not particularly observant about these sort of things but a collection of twelve empty jam pots caught his eye. He was horrified to learn that we had no jam. The next day several jars arrived.

He seemed to me a very powerful man. He could order the fathers of other boys into battle and could produce jam.

Under my father's encouragement I learnt by heart 'Ye Mariners of England who guard our native shores ...' When my father and mother and their important friends came down for the weekends, I was invited to stand up on a stool and recite this poem. I particularly enjoyed the last verse: 'The meteor flag of England shall yet terrific burn, till England's troubled night be passed and the star of Peace return.' I remember this quite vividly and I always thought that I had enjoyed these recitations. But it seems that I bore some resentment against my father in the matter. For my mother has since told me that I used to refer to my father as the 'meteor beast'.

I remember shortly after this there being a lot of people at Lullenden and my father telling them: 'The war will be over very soon.' This must have been the end of October or the beginning of November 1918 when I was seven and a half. A few days later we came back in the pony trap from school, after singing 'O God our help in ages past', and there was the gardener on a ladder nailing up a flag-pole and a Union Jack on one of the chimneys of the house. The Armistice had been declared. That is about all I can remember up to this time except a very horrible nanny called nanny Higgins. I have a feeling that this was before the war when I was only three. I think we were lunching out of doors and there was a mustard pot on the table. I clamoured to have some mustard. Nanny Higgins very properly refused me this condiment. I nagged so much about it that eventually she took a teaspoon, plunged it in the mustard pot, thrust it in my mouth and rattled my teeth with the spoon. This was a cruel thing to do to a young child. I screamed with rage and pain. Diana told my mother and nanny Higgins was sent away.

Two more recollections of Lullenden. A splendid old man with a white beard who looked like King Edward VII came to stay. He was Sir Ernest Cassel and I understood that he had been a great friend of my grandfather's as well as being a friend of my father and mother; also that he was a very rich man. On the morning that he was due to leave, my sister Diana was summoned to see him and came back with a one-pound Treasury note which he had given her. The nanny said: 'Now Sir Ernest wants to see you.' I said, 'Do you think he is going to give me a pound as well?' 'No,' said she, 'I think he's going to give you something bigger.' I was not aware that there was anything bigger than a pound note and somehow or other I had formed the impression that you couldn't give someone two separate pounds, so I approached Sir Ernest with lively interest. He gave me a five-pound note (one of those nice crinkly ones so much superior to the meretricious notes they dish out nowadays). I did not know that such a thing existed and it seemed to me more than all the money in the world. I saw him once more about a year later. Again he gave me a five-pound note. I have never been solvent since.

After the First World War we went, three or four years in a row, to spend Christmas at Blenheim with my father's cousin the Duke of Marlborough. These were always very splendid affairs. Often my godfather Lord Birkenhead was there with his wife and his three children Freddie, Eleanor and Pam. There was always a lot of other children there; the huge park and Palace were wonderful romping grounds.

Christmas 1918 coincided with the end of the War and with the delayed celebrations of the twenty-first birthday of the son and heir Lord Blandford (now Duke of Marlborough). There was a paper-chase on horse-back and a whole ox was roasted. The day concluded with a gigantic bonfire on top of which was placed an effigy of the Kaiser. I seem to remember that F.E.'s daughter, Lady Eleanor Smith, contributed a discarded pair of silk stockings. These were stuffed with straw and served as the Imperial legs. The Kaiser survived for many years and in 1933 I was able to secure an interview with him at Doorn in Holland.

I discussed Sir Ernest's generosity with my governess, Miss Kinsey. She said, 'Well you see, he is a millionaire'. This was the first time I had heard the use of this magic word. She explained to me as best she could what a millionaire was. I asked whether we knew any other millionaires. She said, 'Yes. Colonel and Mrs Spender-Clay who live nearby at Ford Manor. I used to work for them. They are certainly millionaires because Mrs Spender-Clay was an Astor'. 'Don't we know any other millionaires?' I asked. 'Well, your father's friend Sir Philip Sassoon is certainly a millionaire.' I had not then met Philip Sassoon but later I often did, but neither he nor the Spender-Clays ever gave me a fiver.

In the summer of 1919, my father had acquired a barrel of claret. One Sunday Mr Hilaire Belloc drove over with a bottling and corking apparatus to take charge of broaching the barrel. It was tremendous fun. We children carried out the bottles from the barrel to the corking machine. It was a very hot day and we were soon stupefied by the fumes and passed out on the grass. At this moment, some very important people came to call and seemed much shocked by these Bacchanalian scenes: Belloc and my father in their shirt sleeves and the children prone on the grass.

When the war was over my father and mother shared for some months a house called Templeton near Roehampton with my father's cousin, Captain Freddie Guest. There was a huge indoor tennis court. There were many stables full of polo ponies and Richmond Park nearby in which we used to ride the ponies when they were not needed for polo. My father had another birthday here. I don't know if there were any oysters but I remember a very large cake which he cut with a sword. Miss Kinsey was still our governess. She promised me a prize of a George III penny (which looked as large as a cartwheel), when I could read the first leader in *The Times* without a mistake. It was many months before I could manage this task but eventually it was achieved and Miss Kinsey duly gave me the great copper penny which I cherished for many years, but which eventually got lost.

I cannot understand how it was that my father and mother who were always most solicitous of my welfare could have allowed Miss Kinsey to indoctrinate me daily with the political opinions of so pernicious an organ as *The Times*. Perhaps they did not know what was going on, or perhaps they rightly judged that I was too young to be corrupted by the crazy opinions of Lord Northcliffe. Anyway, no harm was done and neither in my early boyhood or later in life have I ever found any difficulty in detecting the essential meretriciousness of the opinions expressed in that paper.

When we were not riding in Richmond Park, we used to go into a neighbouring village (I think called East Sheen) with a very nice nursery maid whose name I do not remember. We used to buy little celluloid swans which we floated in our baths, and on our walks the nursery maid taught me the first popular song that I can remember. It was something out of a popular musical comedy called *The Maid of the Mountains*. It was gloriously sloppy and sentimental, and went something like this: 'What ere befall, I still recall . . .'

Then suddenly I heard that I was to go to boarding school, Sandroyd near Cobham in Surrey. I was excited at the prospect. Though never a dandy in later life I remember very well that what impressed me most were the new clothes that were ordered for this occasion. They came from a firm called Billings & Edmonds. They were all made to measure. There was one suit with knickerbockers, and another with long trousers. Until now I had always worn shorts. They arrived late one evening but I was not allowed to unpack them as it was thought it would excite me unduly. I hardly slept all night. I woke up hours before my usual time and fell on the cardboard boxes and tore the suits out of the lush tissue papers in which they were wrapped. With these lovely clothes it was a treat not a terror to go away to school.

My father had hated most of his school days and he was most concerned about how I would get on. He said to me: 'There is a boy at Sandroyd called Max Aitken. He is the son of a very great friend of mine, Lord Beaverbrook. I am sure you will get on with him very well. Lord Beaverbrook has told his son to keep an eye on you.' I settled down quite happily at Sandroyd but it seemed that a week after I got there I wrote to my father and said, 'You will be sorry to hear that the boy I hate most in the whole school is Max Aitken'. So much for the plans of parents who try to arrange the friendships of their

21

children. I should add that in later life Max Aitken became a friend of mine.

There was a gang of bullies at Sandroyd, organised by two boys older than myself. They held the whole school in awe. They would send their minions to arrest any small boy like myself whom they did not like, and frighten him by swinging and cracking whips around their heads. I cannot recall whether any violence was ever used but it was an alarming process. Many other small boys more inhibited than myself were terrorised and enslaved by this process. Having been brought up with a due respect for law and order, I did not scruple (at the risk of being called a sneak) to denounce the aggressors to the authorities. These proved no more effective (as we were later to find) than did the denunciations of a similar nature to the League of Nations and the United Nations. Throughout my life I have learned that it is better to rely on defensive alliances.

So, with childish prescience of the shape of things to come, I formed a counter-gang to resist these outrages. My gang consisted of a very tough boy called Benn, who I think was a nephew of a Member of Parliament called Sir Arthur Shirley Benn, and three Spanish princes, Alvaro, Alonzo and Atalfo of Orleans-Bourbon. Benn was my Chief of Staff and the three Spanish princes were my bodyguard. We got the better of the older bullies and demoralised them. It was, I must admit, with some satisfaction that I heard a few years later that both our enemies had been sacked from their public schools.

I was on the whole a very good little boy, having been properly brought up by my poor and honest parents. When I first arrived the headmaster, Mr Hornby, said that if one broke anything one must come and own up. A few days after I arrived at the school I broke a small bough off a tree. Slightly with my tongue in my cheek, I suppose, I formed up to the headmaster and confessed to this breakage. He reassured me and told me that matters of such a trivial character were hardly worth reporting. I took comfort from this advice. I never reported anything again.

My greatest friend at Sandroyd was a boy called Rattigan. He also became a member of my counter-gang. In the holidays he would ask me to lunch at his mother's home and we would go and see a matinée, usually a Conan Doyle play about Sherlock Holmes. In the next holidays my mother would ask him back and we would go and see another play. When we left Sandroyd he went to Harrow and I went to Eton, and I didn't see him again for twenty-five years. Meanwhile in the early 'thirties I began to read in the papers about a clever young playwright called Terence Rattigan who had written a play called *French without Tears*. I wondered very much whether it could have been my boyhood friend but it was not until many years later, just after the Second World War when I met him on the *Queen Elizabeth* in Beatrice Lillie's cabin, that I discovered that he was indeed the friend of my youth.

One of the things I remember very well about my four years at Sandroyd was that Queen Marie of Rumania came down to inspect the school. We were all drawn up in two lines on the cricket field. Accompanied by Mr Hornby she inspected all of us. She naturally embraced her three nephews, the Princes Alvaro, Alonzo and Atalfo; she also embraced me. I was flattered but surprised and supposed that she had done this because I was the son of a famous man. I had been indicated to her by Mr Hornby as the son of Mr Churchill. What made us giggle very much was when she also embraced Rattigan, which osculation could not have been due to consanguinity or to the fame of his parents, but was purely a testimonial to his personal charm and good looks.

I suffered one disagreeable experience at Sandroyd when I was about ten years old. There was a young assistant master who made some pretext for me to go and see him in his room. When I got there he made me sit down beside him on the bed. He undid his trousers and caused me to manipulate his organ.

I was much surprised but stood in awe of him and cannot pretend that I found it particularly disgusting, or even that I had any sense of guilt until the housemaid came in without knocking to deliver his laundry. He went scarlet in the face and jumped to his feet rearranging his dress as quickly as he could. I realised then that there was something wrong and took my leave of him as soon as possible. To get back to the main part of the school I had to pass through the swimming bath. There I saw another master, Langdon, who for some reason was called 'Bunch'. The next day the young master said to me, 'Did anyone see you on your way back from my room?' I said, 'Yes, Bunch Langdon did'. 'Well,' he said, 'if he asks you what you were doing say you came to see me about a cricket ball which you had lost and I had found.' At early morning school the next day, Langdon asked me in front of the class what I was doing passing through the swimming bath the evening before last. I am sure that if he had had the good sense to ask me this question privately I would have told him the truth, as I was sure by now that I had been involved in something wrong and wicked. As it was I gave him the facile answer suggested by the young master.

I steered very clear of that young master after this and though the episode had not really left any deep scar on my mind I was puzzled and worried about it. The next summer holidays we went to Rugby. My father had taken the headmaster's house so that he could play polo with his cousin Lord Wimborne nearby at Ashby St Ledgers. We had the use of the school swimming bath and it was there that I learnt to swim. One day I told my sister Diana about this strange experience I had had at Sandroyd. The nanny overheard this and went and reported the matter to my mother, who told my father. I remember very well how my father sent for me one morning when he was still lying in bed and having his breakfast and asked me about the truth of the matter. I told him the truth as I have always done. I don't think I had ever seen him so angry before or since. He leapt out of bed, ordered his car and drove all across country – the round trip must have been well over two hundred miles. He returned late that night. He had seen the headmaster who had told him that the young assistant master had already been dismissed on other grounds. My father said to me, 'Never let anyone do that to you again'. This was the only homosexual experience I ever encountered.

My reports at Sandroyd were nearly all of the 'could do better if he tried' variety. 'He writes slowly and lacks application,' wrote the Mathematics master when I was nine. 'Not so good as he might be' wrote the French master at the same time. 'In written work he is slow and could try more,' wrote the History master. The Headmaster summed up: 'He must develop more concentration before he can make the best of his ability.'

'A quick boy,' wrote the Headmaster a little later: 'at times too quick as he is apt to answer before he thinks.' A year later, when I was ten, he wrote again: 'He likes to dash ahead too fast. He must learn to digest things more slowly and to be tidier.'

Another year later: 'His clumsy pen does not keep up with his quick brain and makes for slipshod work. Sustained concentration will bring him a large measure of success.'

In the following year when I was twelve and a half: 'His thoughts appear to fly from one thing to another with an uncontrolled rapidity that spoils his chances of achieving his best.'

For two or three years after the war we lived in a fine big house in London, No 2 Sussex Square. Our principal recreations were riding in Rotten Row and roller-skating at the rink at Holland Park. One day Diana and I came back from Holland Park and found the house surrounded by policemen. Indoors all sorts of tough-looking men were running up and down the stairs, looking in cupboards, attics and cellars. It was explained to us that earlier in the afternoon Sir Henry Wilson had been assassinated by Irish gunmen on the steps of his house. As my father had been one of the five British signatories of the Irish Treaty there were grounds for supposing that he too might be assassinated. Ever afterwards my father, like the other signatories of the Treaty, usually had a man from the Special Branch of Scotland Yard to look after him. At the beginning, after the first scare, there were three of them.

That summer my father and mother took a house for the summer holidays at Frinton. My father always enjoyed making lakes and damming streams and the three detectives came in very handy on the beaches of Frinton. My father mobilised everybody on the beach and when the tide ran out dammed up the sunken pools left behind and then dug immensely complicated channels to release the stored up water. Sometimes, instead, we would build an enormous sand castle and seek to resist, like latter-day Canutes, the incoming tide.

Another person who had a house at Frinton that summer was Mrs Dudley Ward, and we were very excited when the Prince of Wales came down one day to visit her. She had two very pretty daughters, Penelope and Angie. Penelope is now married to Sir Carol Reed, the film director, and Angie is married to my great friend General Sir Robert Laycock, who later formed the Commandos and was Governor of Malta. Somewhere I have a photograph of me giving a pickaback to Angie. I was eleven and she was three. It makes me realise how old I am getting when I reflect that Angie is now a grand-mother.

There were tennis tournaments at Frinton, and Diana and I were made to enter for them, duffers though we were. We entered for the mixed doubles and were knocked out in the first round by Miss Eileen Bennett and her partner, whose name I don't recall. We won the two booby prizes which were rather handsome – tins shaped like sand buckets, full of Mackintosh's Toffee de Luxe. I think that Miss Bennett, who was then sixteen, was the first woman who stirred my romantic interest. She was very pretty and excited me a great deal. I remember saying to her: 'Do you wear stays, Miss Bennett?' She was taken aback by this question and demanded why I wished to know. I replied: 'I long ago decided that I could never marry a girl who wore stays.' I don't think the matter was pressed further.

My father was always wonderfully spontaneous, resourceful and unexpected in arranging treats for us. One summer, I think it must have been in 1923, we were living in a rented house called 'Hozey Rig' near Chartwell which my father had just bought and which was being rebuilt. This modest villa had been occupied by Lewis Carroll when he was writing *Alice in Wonderland*. My father re-christened it 'Cosy Pig'. My mother and her sister, my Aunt Nellie, were away in Le Touquet. One evening my father arrived from London and asked whether Diana and I would like to accompany him to join my mother and Aunt Nellie at Le Touquet next day. Ho! Were we excited! We could hardly sleep a wink. Next morning we all bundled into the car and drove to Newhaven and made the three-hour crossing to Dieppe. 'I have not told your mother,' said my father, 'it is a surprise.' We all stayed at an hotel for two or three days. We went swimming and Diana and I were allowed into the outer rooms of the casino in the afternoon to watch the Thé Dansant. I am particularly unmusical but even for the unmusical there is a nostalgia in a catching tune and I well remember that it was in the Casino that I first heard the song of the moment: 'Yes, we have no bananas, we have no bananas today.'

When I was about twelve my father asked me whether I would like to go to Eton or Harrow. I thought it was very civilised of him to give me the option. We had been an Etonian family for many generations. My father was only sent to Harrow because it was quaintly thought at the time that he suffered from some lung trouble and that Harrow-on-the-Hill would be better for him than Eton in the fog. Actually lack of lung power has never subsequently been detected in my father, but perhaps it was the salubrious climate of Harrow which rid him of this complaint. My father had not been happy at Harrow. I doubt if he would have been much happier at Eton, but I was greatly complimented that he gave me the choice. I went down and inspected both institutions. It seemed that there were fewer rules and much less discipline at Eton than at Harrow; accordingly I opted for Eton and joined Colonel Sheepshanks' House in October 1924. This was where I was to board for the next four years.

Before I took the Common Entrance Examination my father said he would give me a pony if I took Middle Fourth. I told one of the masters about it and he said 'Does your father mean twenty-five pounds or an animal?' I had not then heard of this distinction. In the event I took Upper Fourth and my father gave me one of his polo ponies, called Ostrich.

A month or so after my arrival at Eton my father was elected with a very large majority as the Constitutionalist Member for Epping and was appointed by Mr Baldwin to be Chancellor of the Exchequer. A year before he had fought the Abbey Division of Westminster against the officially adopted Conservative candidate as an Independent Conservative and had been defeated after three recounts by forty-three votes. I was on holiday at that time and had been allowed to act as telephone operator at 2 Sussex Square where we then lived. I was naturally immensely excited to read of my father's election to Parliament and still more of his unexpected appointment as Chancellor of the Exchequer. I shall never forget how the Captain of the House and the Captain of Games, who of course did not approve of politicians, called upon me in my room and with heavy irony told me how proud they were to have the son of the Chancellor of the Exchequer living under the same roof with them. This was my introduction to the inverted snobbery which unhappily dominates the lives of so many of the upper-middle classes.

PART II: 1924–8

I DID not enjoy Eton very much. I was lazy and unsuccessful both at work and at games. I did not conform to the general pattern and was an unpopular boy. My greatest friend was my second cousin, Tom Mitford. He was about three years older than myself and I learnt a very great deal from him. My sisters and I used to spend quite a lot of our holidays with him and his sisters and they used to come and stay with us at Chartwell. From about the age of fifteen onwards I was very much in love with his sister Diana, who later married Mr Bryan Guinness (now Lord Moyne), and subsequently, Sir Oswald Mosley.

The Mitfords were an extraordinary family. Lord and Lady Redesdale were rather prosaic, humdrum people but they were very kind to all us children. The Mitford children were one of the most varied families I have ever come across. There was one boy, my cousin Tom, and six girls. The eldest, Pamela, I never knew very well and she has now lived for many years in Ireland. Then there was Nancy who has become the highly successful novelist. Then came Diana who was one of the first loves of my life. Then came Unity who later became a great admirer of Hitler. Then there were two younger ones whom I knew much less well, Jessica and Deborah. The family were immensely competitive. When Pamela got engaged to a brewer so did Diana. When Diana and Unity became Fascists Jessica became a Communist and ran away with my cousin Esmond Romilly to the Spanish civil war. Finally Deborah, who had always said that she in contradistinction to her sisters had no interest in politics, announced her intention of being a

Duchess; in due course she became Duchess of Devonshire.

When I got to Sheepshanks' House at Eton one of the great swells in the House was Freddie Furneaux. He was a godson of my father's and I was a godson of his father, Lord Birkenhead. If not then, he soon became the Captain of Games and I was appointed to be his fag. He was a most lenient master. One evening he handed me a hot water bottle and instructed me to fill it and put it in his bed. I did this – or thought that I had done so. The next day he sent for me and said, 'Why didn't you put the hot water bottle in my bed?' I have seldom told a lie in my life; I think lies so dull and the truth is always more interesting. I said I did put it into his bed and he said that it was not there. It was an *impasse*. He said 'Will you do it tonight?' I said, 'Of course'. When I went up to do it that night I realised that the previous night I had put it into the bed in the next-door room. I at once formed up to Lord Furneaux and confessed my error. He complimented me on my candour and said that normally I would have been beaten as he had found it impossible to believe my explanation, but his father (F.E.) under pressure from my father had enjoined him to see that I was never beaten. Thereafter I became a good and assiduous fag, not only to Freddie but to subsequent fag-masters. I thought that everyone came very well out of this episode.

Quite painlessly I was beginning to learn the facts of life and to understand that it was not only honourable but also rewarding to tell the truth as far as you can remember. Of course this does not apply to most newspaper proprietors, editors and their employees. They much prefer to traffic in lies; indeed they have a strong aversion from the truth. This, however, is another story that will emerge in later volumes.

Writing about Freddie reminds me of a splendid fracas he had with our House Tutor, Sheepshanks. The latter was a pocket Hercules somewhat of the build of the late Mr Leopold Amery. One evening while going round the house Sheepshanks had some altercation with Freddie who was at this time

32

RSC: age 3   RSC: age 4

RSC at Miss Violet Asquith's wedding reception after her marriage to Mr Maurice Bonham-Carter, Private Secretary to Mr Asquith, on 30 November 1915, at 10 Downing Street

Back row – l. to r.: Miss Kathleen Tennant (now Kathleen, Duchess of Rutland), Mr Asquith (Prime Minister), the bridegroom, Miss Elizabeth Asquith (later Princess Bibesco)

Front row – l. to r.: Bill Harcourt (later Viscount Harcourt), Michael McKenna, David McKenna, the bride, RSC

As a page at his Aunt
Nellie's wedding to
Colonel Bertram
Romilly

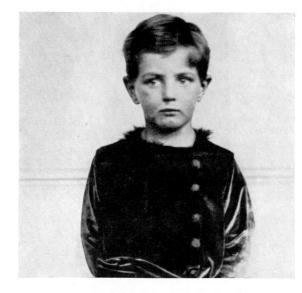

(*below*) Diana
Churchill and RSC
with their cousin
John George
Spencer-Churchill

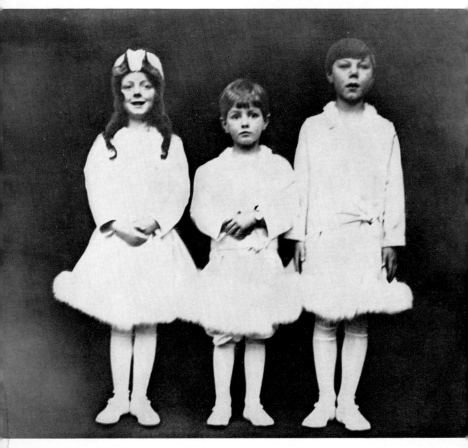

Captain of the House as well as Captain of Games. Playfully Sheepshanks punched Freddie in the chest. Freddie, who was a fine athlete and taller, though less compact than Sheepshanks, punched him back rather harder. Sheepshanks made to hit Freddie again. By this time tempers were aroused; Freddie tackled Sheepshanks, pushed him down the stairs and they rolled down two or three flights in a very noisy fashion. On each flight the boys opened their doors and looked out to see what the commotion was. Fortunately no bones were broken but everybody at M'tutors felt that Freddie was very much 'one up'. He didn't have very much rot from Sheepshanks thereafter; and nor did I, though for different reasons.

Shortly before, Freddie, who by now was Captain of the House, Captain of Games, Keeper of the Field and President of Pop and had earned every title to glory which an athlete could win, proposed me for membership of the 'debate'. This was largely an office of dignity and did not possess so much power or authority as did 'The Library,' but we did meet once a week or once a fortnight to debate various issues such as 'Capital Punishment' and 'Free Trade' which are often the staple discussions of young men.

There was a good deal of opposition to my election; but Freddie pushed me in. He said 'This is not a popularity contest; we surely want to encourage people who are articulate and have the power of speech'.

I cannot recall what interventions I made during debates; but as a result of being elected I had the privilege of hearing Freddie's moving speech to the house debating society which was traditionally made on the departure of the Head of House. It seemed that he had little more respect for our tutor than I had and he wound up the spirited peroration by saying that Colonel Sheepshanks reminded him of something that had been written about Henry VIII. I don't think it was particularly relevant but I was immensely impressed by his power to recite this without any notes.

Freddie's quotation was thuswise: 'This monarch was sincere, open, gallant, liberal, intrepid, inflexible and courageous; but with these virtues he combined the vices of violence, cruelty, profusion, rapacity, obstinacy, injustice, arrogance, presumption and conceit.' When I got to Oxford and more or less caught up with him I asked him the source of the quotation. He replied evasively: 'I had it from the headmaster of my private school, but he did not disclose where it came from.'

At Eton there was a curious rule quite different I believe from other public schools about beatings of the boys: the Headmaster could swipe the upper boys, the lower master could swipe the lower boys. None of the other masters was allowed to beat the boys.

In each House, however, the Captain of the House and the Captain of Games had this privilege. But it was exercised in a civilised manner – perhaps all the more frightening for this. At 9.10, just after prayers which concluded our daily devotions, the Captain of Games who had opened 'The Library' door would shout 'Boy'. The last boy to arrive was always entrusted with the errand. Freddie had now left and I was no longer a fag, so four or five possible delinquents who did not know whether their delinquencies had been discovered or not, waited in apprehension in their rooms. Two or three times at least a knock would come on my door and a little boy looking rather frightened would come in and say 'Churchill, you're wanted in "The Library",' Prepared for the worst but resolved to maintain my dignity as best I could (I would have been about fifteen at this time) I went downstairs at a measured tread seething with anxiety and potential indignation.

There were six or seven members in 'The Library'. 'The Library' did not consist of more than two or three dozen books and half a dozen newspapers. On entry one was confronted with the Captain of the House or the Captain of Games. One or other of these potentates would be standing up swishing with a cane. Behind him sat in a semicircle the four or five other members of 'The Library'. Behind this 'bumph', as all forms of paper were indiscriminately described, were decently concealed the other four or five members of 'The Library'. (They were in fact the equivalent in other schools of prefects.)

They studiously took no part in this procedure. The potentate of the House stated the charge of which I had been accused. This was seldom the work of a private informer. We all had to do so many 'times' per week, ie to take some form of exercise. The least irksome for me was to take a run. This, even loping along, scarcely consumed more than thirty minutes of precious leisure for the sake of which after all I had exercised the option my father had offered me of going to Eton or Harrow in favour of the former. One had to write one's name on a list on a notice-board outside 'The Library'; sometimes the charge was merely that of having forgotten to sign one's name. This was venial. Sometimes, however, it was alleged that I had filled in a 'Time' fraudulently. This was much more grave. I don't think that I ever did this. However, on the occasion which I have in mind this was the charge preferred against me. There seemed to be no evidence for the charge and I indignantly rebutted it. My remonstrances were of no avail. The Captain of Games was as implacable as Minos. He said 'Anyway you have been bloody awful all round – bend down, you're going to have six up'.

Such was the rough justice at Eton. I do not think it had any bad effect on me and I do not think it turned me into a juvenile delinquent, nor do I suppose that it deterred me: I took it for granted.

When I came upstairs again many anxious commiserating heads popped out from their rooms, vastly relieved to see me returning with an angry but a cheerful face.

There was one occasion when I was up before 'The Library' and I was bitterly resentful of its injustice because I was guiltless. The Captain of the House by this time was a boy called

Southby, the son of the MP for Epsom, Commander Archibald Southby.

Southby was of handsome appearance and a fine athlete; but he did not like me and I didn't like him. At this period in my life (I was fifteen or sixteen) I was not nearly as articulate as I am today, and when I strove to express myself and could not find the words I needed I went red in the face and tears – not of fear, but of frustration – came to my eyes. Southby, however, was a just boy, and realised that I was telling the truth. For once I was acquitted and went scot-free.

This must have been the summer half. I had joined the Officers Training Corps and we all went off to camp. It was Southby's last half, and the cameraderie of an open-air life under disagreeable conditions bridged the gulf in age, and I had the opportunity of thanking him for his sense of justice. He told me that our tutor, Colonel Sheepshanks, with whom he had discussed the matter, had recommended him to beat me. I was aghast at this duplicity on Sheepshanks' part – he who had always purported to be my friend and protector.

So when I came back next half, I determined to have my revenge. Sheepshanks used to come round on his periodic visitations after prayers to talk to the boys in our individual rooms as we were going to bed; when he came to me I treated him with cold disdain. This seemed to rattle him and after four or five nightly visits he said, 'What's the matter Churchill, why won't you talk to me?' I told him what the matter was; that he, without consulting me or knowing the facts, had urged a boy who had no reason to like me into an act of injustice. I never had much trouble with Sheepshanks after this. He kept his distance.

One night when I was about sixteen Sheepshanks said to me, 'Why are you seeing so much of Mercer-Nairne? [Later Marquess of Lansdowne and a Minister of State at the Foreign Office.] He is two years younger than you and in another House'. I replied, 'What on earth sir, can it have to do with you?' He replied, 'You must be aware of the biblical text, "But whoso shall offend one of these little ones which believe in me, it were better for him that a millstone were hanged about his neck, and that he were drowned in the depth of the sea".' I said, 'It seems to me sir, that you are making an accusation against me of unnatural vice. If you say such a thing to anyone else I will see to it that you are sued for slander'. He was much abashed and realised that he had got off on the wrong foot. I added, 'Though it's none of your business, sir, you may be interested to know that the reason I see so much of Mercer-Nairne is that I happen to be in love with his sister'. I never had any more rot from Sheepshanks who subsequently found himself at a grave disadvantage in all his transactions with me.

I was very romantic at this period of my life, and I carefully preserved all the letters from the girls I loved. I find from a reference to Margaret Mercer-Nairne's letters that the conduct of well brought-up young ladies was far more strict than it is today. When Margaret and I were seventeen I was allowed to take her out to tea, but not to luncheon. And of course dinner and night-clubs were quite out of the question. These regulations were sternly enforced by Margaret's mother, Lady Violet Astor (later Lady Astor, wife of the 1st Baron Astor of Hever, of Hever Castle, not to be confused with Viscountess Astor of Hever Castle). Margaret lived with her mother and stepfather at Hever Castle, only seven or eight miles from Chartwell, so there was always a lot of coming and going between the two houses.

Later Margaret transferred her affections to my cousin Tom Mitford, who was my greatest friend. I have never believed in men friends quarrelling about girls: after all, there are plenty to go round. Margaret was very much in love with Tom and I sought to be the good angel of the romance. One evening, when I was at Chartwell, Margaret rang up and said that she had written a most imprudent letter to Tom which she was afraid would infuriate him. She said that Tom was away in the West country but that she had sent the letter to his small London flat, Rutland Gate Mews, where Tom often put me up when I was in London. She asked me to retrieve the letter: I agreed to undertake this extravagant and somewhat exorbitant demand.

I had no car of my own at this time, but staying with us was Alan Lennox-Boyd (now Viscount Boyd of Merton), a friend of my sister Diana's. I pressed him into service. At seven in the morning he drove me to London. He waited in the car while I rang the bell. The door was opened by Tom's admirable house-keeper, Mabel, whom I knew well. I affected surprise when she said that Tom was not back from the country. I asked if I could come in and scribble a note to him. I was admitted and went up to his sitting room. There, sure enough, on a table, was his morning's mail. There were three letters: among them I readily detected Margaret's. I slipped it into my pocket, sat down and wrote a hasty note to Tom, saying that I was sorry to have missed him, took my leave of Mabel and rejoined Alan in his car. We were back at Chartwell by 9.30 in time for breakfast. I immediately telephoned Margaret that my mission was accomplished. She was overcome with gratitude. I asked if, as a reward, I might read the letter. She said, 'No, burn it'. This I honourably did.

I had wondered whether Mabel would have noticed my theft. Sure enough, she had: it was a pity that Tom did not have a larger mail that morning. About lunchtime Tom rang up and asked what it was that I had stolen. I explained that I had been acting under Margaret's orders. The incident caused no breach between us. It seems that in those early days I was much given to acts of chivalry and gallantry. My sister Diana used fancifully to recall (though I do not recollect it) that at one time Lady Violet barred me from Hever as she had higher ambitions for her daughter. Accordingly, one night I swam the moat and kept a midnight assignation with Margaret in the medieval torture chamber in the castle.

Another brush that I had at this time with Colonel Sheepshanks concerned Virginia Woolf's novel *Orlando*. I can't recall how old I was at the time, but he was deeply shocked at seeing it in my room and only slightly mollified when I told him that the book had been lent to me by my father who had recommended me to read it. It was dreadfully easy to score off Colonel Sheepshanks. Thirty or forty years later I bought a King Charles Cavalier Spaniel from Mrs Paul Maze who had bred him. He, for some reason I have never understood, was called in the stud book 'Urlandu'. I immediately rechristened him 'Orlando' because of his slightly epicene characteristics, and today he is the delight and joy of my household. Often when I look at him I think of Colonel Sheepshanks.

The headmaster, Dr Alington, always treated me with great civility. He would usually invite me to breakfast one Sunday each half. He usually had seven or eight boys each week. Breakfast was very much superior to what we had at my tutor's. Also, I made friends with his daughters, Kathleen and Elizabeth. The latter is now married to Sir Alec Douglas-Home. Sometimes they used to ask ten or twelve of the boys in to supper and a sing-song on Saturday or Sunday evenings. We used to sing songs like 'Green Grow the Rushes, O!' and old fashioned music hall songs like 'I've got a Motto, Always Merry and Bright'.

Dr Alington, who subsequently became Dean of Durham, was an exceptionally handsome man with a very fine presence. He was not popular either with the boys or with the masters. The boys blasphemously used to call him 'Creeping Christ'; the masters were disadvantaged by the ironic wit with which he would frequently regale them. Encountering a newly arrived and earnest young master in the school yard, Dr Alington observed:

'I have just been lecturing to the boys in the sixth form about the Sermon on the Mount.'

'Oh really, Dr Alington. What did you have to tell them?'

'I explained that it was a lot of uncommon nonsense.'

'Oh really, Sir! How do you mean?'

'Well, you wouldn't call it commonsense would you?'

Dr Alington had a commonplace-book in which he had collected many unusual anecdotes and epigrams. I remember him showing me one which greatly struck my fancy:

> The doors to success are always ajar.
> And the entrance halls are full.
> And some get in by the door marked Push,
> And some by the door marked Pull.

I remember repeating this to my mother. She was shocked by the cynical levity of the Headmaster.

When I was about sixteen I was confirmed in the Church of England. I was carefully prepared for this ceremony and took it very seriously. However, shortly after I had been confirmed and had taken my first Communion, I began to have serious doubts. I could not understand how it was possible to reconcile the omnipotence of the Deity with the doctrine of free will. I took the opportunity, one breakfast with the Headmaster, who was a Doctor of Divinity, to raise this problem with him. He treated the matter with such inconsequential frivolity that I am sorry to say I lost my faith. I have been trying to regain it ever since.

The first Classics master who I was 'up to' at Eton was a singularly formidable looking man known as 'Briny' Brinton. Despite his menacing appearance he was a euphorist. When our division, as classes were called at Eton, assembled for the first time he introduced himself to us with a short speech which ended with the lines 'The world is so full of a number of things that I'm sure we shall all be as happy as kings'. He was apt to repeat this quotation on any occasion which seemed to him suitable.

I was up to Brinton in a large, gloomy old room that was known as Lower School. Here was the famous birching block where Lower boys were birched. These events provided the late

Monsignor Ronald Knox with an apt allusion in some re-markably precocious verse which he wrote at the age of fourteen. It was inspired by some improvements that were being made at the time in School Yard, and began:

> Powers of the Bursary who on a cursory
> Glance at the ruinous state of School Yard,
> Made us to travel securely on gravel –
> Is not that gravel a little too hard?
> Does not the scenery call for some greenery?
> Call for a garden in which we might lop
> Calceolarias of suitable areas,
> Worthy to rest on the bosoms of Pop?

He goes on to describe the amenities he envisaged:

> Where with disaster, the stern lower master,
> Urges the fugitive footsteps of sin
> Prickly acacias surround the embrasures
> Screening the coveted vision within.

Another famous Eton master that I was 'up to' a little later on was 'Tuppy' Headlam. He was, I think, the brother of a bishop and of Sir Cuthbert Headlam who represented some North-country constituency for many years in the House of Commons. Tuppy was a very endearing character. He conducted his division with a long-established ritual to which everybody contributed to give him gratification and so waste as much time as possible. For instance, if it were possible for any boy to ask the question, 'Please sir, how long has this been going on?' everybody would chant together while Tuppy would smile benignantly:

'Day after day, week after week, month after month, year after year, lustre after lustre, decade after decade, century after century, millenium after millenium, ice age after ice age, wood pulp age after wood pulp age, eternity after eternity.' This took all of two minutes to get through and everybody felt most relaxed at the end of it, not the least Tuppy.

He was supposed to be teaching us Classics but most of us tended to resist the process. When, for instance, Tuppy said to me, 'Churchill, will you go on to construe?' I would reply, 'Sir, where should I start?' The whole division would chant together: 'You will start at the beginning, you will go on to the end and then you will stop.' This gave one time to consult one's nearest neighbour as to the probable translation of at least the first sentence of the matter that had to be turned viva voce from Latin into English which one was supposed with blind optimism to have prepared in advance.

There had been two boys who had been 'up to' Tuppy a couple of years before me. Their names were Primrose and Hare. One was the grandson of Lord Rosebury; the other is the recent Chairman of the Conservative party, Lord Blakenham. They were always referred to as Flora and Fauna.

Tuppy was the lineal academic descendant of one of the most famous of all Eton masters, Austen Leigh. Of him it was related that he went with another Eton schoolmaster on a walking tour to the Lake District. Arriving at some wayside railway station (probably now closed down by that admirable man Dr Beeching) Austen Leigh had an altercation with the stationmaster which concluded with Leigh saying with great emphasis and anger: 'I shall write to the stationmaster in Milan about this.' His friend and colleague was too timid to ask immediately the relevance of this retort. They walked up the mountains and eventually sat down to eat their sandwiches. When it seemed that Austen Leigh's anger had abated his youthful colleague made bold to ask the significance of this remark. Austen Leigh replied, still with some asperity, 'Forty years ago I had a row with the stationmaster in Milan and I told him that if ever I met a stupider stationmaster than him I would write and let him know. I now propose to do so.'

There were two other eccentric Eton masters of whom I saw less than I did of Briny Brinton and Tuppy Headlam, but they were already legendary figures, Luxmoore and Broadbent. Luxmoore was thin and had white hair not unlike that distinguished charlatan Bertrand Russell. Broadbent exactly lived

up to his name. He suffered I suppose from sciatica and walked
in an ungainly fashion with the support of two sticks, and he
had the largest bottom I have ever seen. Broadbent had one
other distinction. He had beaten Mr Asquith for the Ireland
scholarship in 1873 and was bracketed with Asquith as the
winner of the Craven in 1874. These two men, both of them I
suppose in their seventies, were deadly but amiable enemies.
One day after chapel Broadbent hobbled up to Luxmoore and
said, 'Do you realise that today is St George's Day?' 'Of course
I do,' retorted Luxmoore in a testy fashion, 'after all I am
President of the Shakespeare Society.' 'Well, it isn't,' said
Broadbent. History does not recall what revenge Luxmoore
practised on Broadbent.

Luxmoore, who must have been a man of some means, had
acquired a small island perhaps of an acre's extent in one of
the by-waters of the Thames. From it there was a most splendid
view of Eton Chapel. He lavished his care upon it and used to
allow a limited number of boys access to it. I was made free
of the garden by my friend and cousin Tom Mitford who always
called it Jardin de Luxe.

There I spent many happy hours reading Keats and Shelley.
There I saw my first kingfisher flitting over the narrow channel
that divided the garden from the mainland. It added an exclu-
sive oasis of charm to what had been for four centuries an
ancient seat of civilisation and learning. One hardly ever found
more than three or four other boys there. It was a divine spot
for reading and meditation. One crossed a small wooden
bridge to gain access to this latter-day garden of Eden. There
was a little notice by a wicket gate written in Luxmoore's own
handwriting in Greek: 'Dogs and beggars keep out.' There
was also a printed Latin tag: 'Amici et Amicorum' (for my
friends and their friends).

There was an ancient institution or practice at Eton known
as the 'saying lesson'. Each week every boy, from the time of
his entry, was required to learn ten lines of prescribed poetry by

heart and to recite them at the moment ordained by the masters. I found quite soon that I had an appetite for this and that I could learn the lines very quickly. One of the few points of self-discipline in which I indulged at Eton was to learn ten lines of poetry, or a sonnet – fourteen lines – each night before lights out. I found it got easier and easier and nearly everything I taught myself then I can still remember. After a bit I found it rather irksome to have to learn the pre-ordained lines selected by the masters and I sought permission to recite once a week lines of my own choice. Permission for this was readily granted; thus I could read what I liked and not only just what was imposed on myself and the other boys.

I do commend to all parents the obligation of reading aloud in the home circle and of encouraging children, if necessary with bribes, to learn poetry by heart. Nothing can give them a more felicitous command of their own language. This is one of the most precious endowments which parents, however poor, can bequeath to their children.

At Eton my reports were no better than they had been at Sandroyd. At first my Mathematical tutors seemed to be the most percipient: 'He is hideously ingenious for a boy of his years,' wrote Mr A. G. Huson, when I was fourteen. 'I hope this bodes well for the Country. I must say he is extremely good fun; one does not talk much when he wants to.'

A little later, the Mathematics master, Mr H. G. Babington Smith reported 'Obstinacy appears to be one of his more prominent characteristics. He has shown himself to be possessed of a natural capacity in many directions but he does not take kindly to being taught.'

Mr Badcock reported with some accuracy when I was not yet fifteen: 'A talkative youth with a merry disposition. Works fairly but not much good at Maths.'

Mr Kerry reporting on me when I was nearly sixteen and when I was fourteenth out of fourteen in my Division wrote: 'The reason for this humble result is not entirely that he is the worst mathematician in the Division – though I think it probable that he is. But he is further handicapped by his obsession for the sound of his own voice. At first I dared to answer him back (in fear and trembling) but, finding I was not completely withered, I persevered and have managed to keep his effusiveness slightly in check. It has been good fun (but poor Maths).'

My classical teachers were less indulgent. Mr Harford complained when I was fourteen: 'His chief fault at present is to strain to breaking point a natural adroitness of mind by indulging in constant interruptions in the form of queries and quibbles. He shews at present no sign of realising that one of the best forms of discrimination and to develop criticism is self-criticism, a faculty which would enable him to see that his remarks, wasteful of time and fraying to everyone's patience, are very largely cheap, pointless and irrelevant.'

It was not until I began to specialise in history that my interest in work was partially stimulated. Mr C. R. N. Routh reported for the Lent half of 1928 when I was not yet seventeen:

'After ten weeks in a history division with Churchill, I am afraid I am still a little doubtful what to write about him. He seems to me to be a boy whose ideas and ambitions have outrun his years and capacities. Much of his work is very poor in character, but one is led to look for something better by the flashes which not seldom light up the rest of his work, and one forgets that he is below the average age of the division.

'My chief criticism is that at present Churchill has very little use for mere facts. He is obsessed with the beauty of theories, but he forgets that historical theories without facts to prove his theories are mere vapourings. And it is this almost scorn for facts which leads people to think that he does less work than he really puts in. He has only had one failure this Half with me, but with most other boys three or four of his essays must have meant a "tear-over". I am a little frightened that

Churchill may not turn his gifts to advantage unless he can bring himself to do some drudgery.

'And that he has some gifts even his poorest work proves. He brings to his history what very few other boys bring – ardent enthusiasm. He is overflowing with ideas, he has passionate likes and hates, he is as courageous as they make them in defending his theories, and he has a dialectical skill which is often needed if he is going to get out of some of the holes into which he gets himself. But he does get out of them!

'His literary style is lively and bold. It often degenerates into melodrama, but it is always interesting and always fresh. He has more sense of balance and rhythm in prose than anyone else in the division, so that I have always turned to his work with relief. But some of the views that he expresses are too reactionary even for me!

'Altogether I have enjoyed making his acquaintance, and I hope to meet him again. Is it unkind – it is not meant to be – to suggest that he is too quarrelsome, that he likes being in a minority, and enjoys, not rubbing people up the wrong way, but the result of having rubbed them the wrong way?'

The most percipient of my tutors, however, was probably Mr Robert Birley, who was later to become Headmaster of Charterhouse and of Eton, 1949–64. He wrote the following report to my House tutor Sheepshanks in July 1928, just before I finally left Eton:

Let it be said at once that his work was not always satisfactory. There was a period when he seemed to be reading the books extremely sketchily, though he certainly improved in this, and he is very careless about showing up his work in time. But he answers fairly well to expostulation. He is not by any means a bad worker, and there is all the difference between a boy who takes a holiday and then does nothing, and one who reads widely and does not waste his time. But he needs discipline and he must not get into the habit of working only when he wants to.

His real trouble is his facility. He finds it a great deal too easy to do moderately well, and he is developing too early the journalist's ability to 'work up' a little information or a solitary idea. I can give a good, though rather an unfair, example. The other day, when he was with me we talked for five or ten minutes about Shaftesbury, and I told him one or two points. The next morning one of the questions in the trial paper was on Shaftesbury's career. As he is up to me in trials I happened to look at his paper and saw that he had done the question. He had served up just the few things I had said, turned into a longish answer. It was extremely well done. There were some excellent allusions and the whole thing was thrown into the form of a good summary of his character.

The trouble is it was far too well done. There is nothing wrong in his putting down the ideas given him or in his expanding them. But for all the allusions and the good writing there really was hardly any original thought or real thought at all in the whole answer. It was, in fact, a piece of very good journalism.

There is no need for him merely to do this. He has a first-rate brain. But he must be prepared to do some hard thinking for himself and not to take an easy course. His easy course will not be a dull one, in fact it will be an amusing and interesting one. But it will be second-rate for all that.

There is one other matter which is a little disquieting. He seems to find his friends entirely among people who are either more stupid or much younger than himself. I am really more worried about the former. He really must not search out foils. It is far too easy a way to be clever. This fact is due, of course, to the difficulty he finds to get on with his contemporaries. Here I think he has shown great improvement. Knowing that he was likely to become unpopular in any division he was in, I was rather uneasy about mine this half. But he behaved really well, without aggressiveness and conceit. This is a very good sign. I am asking him to join the Essay Society, which should I think be useful to him.

I have attacked him pretty often about his style, though I am not really very alarmed about it. It is at the moment abominable, extremely rhetorical, windy and involved, full of clichés and pomposity. All these, however, are faults on the right side. They are due partly to his reading a good deal of Macaulay, mostly to an attempt on his side to form a style (which is to be commended). I think that he should try to get out of it and write more simply. It makes his answers now very heavy and rather jaded.

He is trying I think to improve his handwriting, but not very steadily. He must persevere in this. He is quite one of the most interesting pupils I have had, and he is a very pleasant one. His mind is very vigorous and his interests are wide. At the moment he is going through a mental crisis. I consider it almost inevitable that a boy with a mind as logical as his should experience very real religious difficulties. It is almost a sign of mental honesty. But while it is good that he should be honest in this, and that he should be ambitious, I hope he will not become too self-centred. There *is* a danger of this.

While I was at Eton Brendan Bracken began to play a large part in the family circle. I first met him when he was helping my father at the by-election in the Abbey division of Westminster in January 1924 when my father was beaten by forty-three votes. I very well remember his first arrival at Chartwell. I suppose I was a boy of twelve or thirteen. My father was building a house in the trees for us children. He was half-way up a large lime tree. Brendan arrived and I was sent down to meet him. I said to him, 'Good afternoon Mr Bracken'. At this time he had not got sufficient self-confidence to realise what an advantage the name Brendan was to prove to him. So he replied 'Call me Peter'. Later I repeated this to Eddie Marsh who told me the story of some lady who appeared to be pressing her claims on the late Lord Beatty (whose name was David) and kept calling him Peter. Someone said to another who was at the party, 'Why does she keep calling him Peter?' 'I suppose,' was the reply, 'because he denied her thrice.'

My father and mother, though busy people, always took trouble about us children, particularly in the holidays. From the time I was about twelve we went abroad nearly every summer. Usually we motored through France in a bumbling old Wolseley limousine. Often 'Prof' Lindemann would accompany us in his glamorous Mercedes-Benz. One year I remember we went to Biarritz and then drove all along the northern foothills of the Pyrenees to Carcassone and the French Riviera.

During my first year at Eton my father took me on a particularly exciting expedition. He and my uncle Jack and I travelled overland to Genoa where we caught a big steamer which stopped for four or five hours the next day at Naples. We drove off to see the ruins of Pompeii. I was not allowed to accompany my father and Uncle into the newly-discovered ruins of Herculaneum with the indecent pictures on the walls.

RSC playing
tennis at Frinton:
1922

RSC with Diana
and Sarah: age 10,
January 1922

RSC and Mary with Diana Mitford: age 13

Diana and RSC with friends. *l. to r.:* Diana, RSC, Diana Mitford, Bryan Guinness (later Lord Moyne), Alan Lennox-Boyd (later Viscount Boyd of Merton)

I had to remain above ground, kicking my heels. I remember we were late getting back to Naples. I was dreadfully worried that we would miss the boat. My father seemed to have no anxiety and it was still there when we arrived at the docks. Next morning we arrived at 7.30 in the Straits of Messina. There a destroyer sent by my father's old friend, Admiral Sir Roger Keyes, at that time Commander-in-Chief, Mediterranean, was waiting for us. We stepped aboard and four hours later arrived in Malta. We spent the weekend there and my father on Saturday played his last game of polo. He was fifty-one at the time. On Monday we sailed in HMS *Warspite* with the whole Mediterranean Fleet and had three days and nights of wonderfully exciting naval exercises. We then arrived and anchored in the Piraeus. We disembarked at once and drove to the Parthenon where we all had a picnic luncheon while my father painted a picture. That night we embarked in another destroyer, sailed through the Corinth Canal and arrived the following afternoon at Brindisi where we caught the night train for Rome.

Here we had four very exciting days. We saw the Colosseum, the Forum, St Peter's, the Pope, and Mussolini, the latter at a reception at the British Embassy where we were staying. During the next few years there were three separate attempts to murder Mussolini. I remember that my father was beginning to exhaust his stock of congratulatory telegrams on the Duce's preservation; soon, however, the attempts ceased. Of course, we did not then know how tiresome this Socialist dictator was subsequently to prove.

A lot of careful protocol went into the private audience which my father and I had with Pope Pius. As an important minister serving under a Protestant sovereign my father felt that he ought not to kneel, but everything was arranged very easily. We were told that we should treat His Holiness merely as a temporal sovereign and bow to him three times: once at the door, once half-way and once when we arrived at his desk. All this passed off very well. The early part of the conversation was a little sticky. Then my father and the Pope got on to the subject of the Bolsheviks and had a jolly half-hour saying what they thought of them. I had stuffed my pockets with a lot of statuettes of the Madonna and Child which I thought would make acceptable gifts for my Catholic friends if they could be blessed by the Pope. My father detected them on the way to the Vatican and said that I must on no account reveal them. However, when we were taking our leave my father suggested that His Holiness should bless me, though he asked no such benediction for himself.

The Pope rose from his seat for the occasion, placing his right hand on my head and a few seconds later his left hand on my father's. Recognising my father's Protestant scruples, he said, 'This is just the blessing of an old man and you can both take it in any spirit that you choose'. He then said a few words in Latin which I fear neither my father nor myself were able to understand. It was very moving and I felt that my statuettes had also been blessed, though I had not revealed them to His Holiness. I was also presented with a silver medal, which I have since seen it falsely stated I sold on my return to Eton. It seems to have disappeared but I am quite sure that I did not 'pop' it.

One summer, when I was about fourteen, my father and mother took all us children up to Holker, to spend ten days with Lord Richard and Lady Moyra Cavendish. My father spent most of the time damming streams.[1] Holker, which is on the west coast of Lancashire, is a most attractive residence. When it was time for me to return to Eton, a day or two ahead of the rest of my family, I was driven to the station, all of twenty-five miles away, by Lady Cranborne (now Lady Salisbury), the daughter of the house. When we got to the station, I thanked her profusely for her kindness in driving me so great a distance and I said, 'Lady Cranborne, thank you so much'. She said,

---

[1] I have a photograph showing me assisting him in these operations.

'Don't be silly; call me Betty'. This I think was the first time that I became conscious of the emotion of romantic love.

It was immensely flattering to be invited to call a grown-up woman by her christian name. When, a few months later, I happened to be talking to my father and mother about our visit to Holker and referred to Lady Cranborne as Betty, I was sharply reproved for my impertinence. I had the satisfaction of telling them that she had invited me to do so. I have cherished a warm spot for her ever since, though I do not always agree with her political opinions, or with those of her husband.

To prevent boys going beyond the authorised limits there was in the afternoon at Eton a roll-call which, with typical Eton illogicality, was called 'Absence'. When your name was called you indicated your presence by raising your hat and shouting 'Sir!' It was almost a point of honour with boys of spirit to break bounds and get away from Eton. The most adventurous liked to go to Windsor races, or still more, to Ascot races. During Ascot week extra Absences were ordained to make it harder. Moreover some of the masters used to go to the races; this added to the hazards of the undertaking. Some boys of exceptional spirit used to climb out at night and drive to London and spend a gay evening in a night-club. The penalty if detected was certainly being 'swiped' by the Headmaster with a birch, and possibly being sacked. I was a prudent boy in many ways but thought that I owed it to my sense of morale to make at least some limited breach of the rules. Accordingly with a young colleague, Stephen Cohen, I walked to Slough and caught a train at about one o'clock in the afternoon to London. We had put on tidy sports clothes under our over-coats and crushed soft homberg hats in our pockets, with which, at the appropriate moment, to replace our school caps. We had arranged that two other boys on the fringe of the crowd would cry 'Sir!' when our names were called at 2.30 pm. We had to be back for 'lock-up' at 6.30 pm.

The expedition had no serious object save to prove to our-

51

selves that we could evade the vigilance of the school authorities. When we got to Paddington we didn't quite know what to do; so we took a taxi to Gunter's Teashop in Berkeley Square and had strawberry icecreams. Then, as we were at a loose end, I rang my sister Diana at 11 Downing Street, where we then lived. She said that my father and mother were both out and suggested that we go round and have tea with her. This we did. Scarcely were we in her sitting room when my mother came in. My friend and I hid behind the curtains. Soon we hurried home to Eton and got back in plenty of time. There was still the anxiety as to whether we had got away with it or not at 'Absence'. By some chance the master in charge omitted to call my name and the boy who was answering for my friend was of small stature and was not detected in the crowd. We felt we had been very brave and resourceful; we told our closest friends and gathered a fugitive admiration for our exploit. But I saw no need to repeat it.

I had a friend in another House called George Lewis who had been at my preparatory school. He was the son of the famous Sir George Lewis, the great Edwardian solicitor of the firm Lewis & Lewis. Young George was a lively boy and he confided to me how he rigged up an early radio set in his room – radios were, of course, strictly forbidden. He came round to my room and helped me to do the same. The aerial was put round the top of the picture rail, came down behind a curtain, and went into the bottom of a basket chair. Underneath we installed a piece of 3-plywood on which the set could rest, and in the seat of the chair cut a small trap door (concealed by a cushion) through which one could manipulate the cat's whisker of this early crystal set, and where one could also conceal the headphones. The set worked beautifully and I had far more fun listening to the BBC in those circumstances than I have ever had since. In 1926 when I was about fifteen, I heard on my earphones the news of the end of the General Strike. I have always enjoyed imparting news. Having replaced the receiver of my headphones and disconnected the cat's whisker, I rushed out of my room. But hardly had I passed the threshold than I realised how dangerous it would be to do so.

I hurried down town and on my return a few moments later, communicated my intelligence to one and all, pretending that I had garnered it from some shopkeeper in the town. Later, of course, in the Second World War, underground receiving stations were to become very numerous; but I like to think that the two sets George Lewis and I operated at Eton were the pioneers.

At Eton it was virtually obligatory to join the Officers Training Corps. If it had been voluntary, as it is now, I expect a lot of boys would have joined it and taken it seriously. As it was, nearly everyone, including, I fear, myself, treated it as a joke. At the end of the summer half in 1928 we went into camp for a week at Tidworth. One morning, some ten of us cadets were in a tent being instructed in the rudiments of the art of signalling by a sergeant in the Regular Army when a messenger came in and said, 'Private Churchill to report at once to the Adjutant'. I repaired to his tent in haste, wondering what breach of discipline I had committed. He handed me a signal which read:

War Office. Camp Commandant from Secretary of State for War. Most immediate, clear the line. Mr Winston Churchill Chancellor of the Exchequer will be visiting Tidworth on Sunday and would like to take his son out to lunch.

It later transpired that my father had been having lunch with the Secretary of State for War, Sir Laming Worthington-Evans. My father had boasted, as fathers are apt to do, that his son was in camp at Tidworth. 'Do you think I could go down and see him?' my father asked. 'Certainly,' replied 'Worthy', 'I will arrange it myself.'

The signal arrived about midnight, the Adjutant had to be aroused to decipher it and the Colonel commanding the camp had to be informed of this item of news. It did not make me popular. I have never been able to cure my father of his life-long habit of what he calls 'Doing business with people at the top'. Indeed I have tended to adopt the same rule myself, but I try to avoid it as far as my children are concerned.

Meanwhile there was to be a Tattoo on the Friday night which all the corps was invited to attend. A few volunteers were called for to look after the camp, and to prepare cocoa for their comrades against their return. I had already seen a number of Tattoos, so I volunteered to remain behind. Another who did so was my great new friend Seymour Berry, now 2nd Viscount Camrose. He is two years older than me and took the Corps very seriously. He was a Company Quartermaster-sergeant. He had to stay behind in any case to supervise the cocoa. After the main body had marched away to the Tattoo, and we had made the necessary preliminary arrangements about cocoa, Seymour and I walked up on to the Downs which overlooked not only the camp but also the Tattoo ground. From the Downs, we could get a fine distant view of the Tattoo without the labour of marching to it in formation. I remember that evening vividly because it was then that Seymour introduced me to the delights of Omar Kayyam, a poet with whose work I was not yet familiar and who has been a constant source of pleasure to me throughout my life.

On our return to camp both our names were taken. Neither of us had been conscious of any infraction of orders in going a few hundred yards out of camp. We thought that, so long as we arranged the cocoa, we had done all right. However, the next morning we were summoned to the Orderly Room and were severely reprimanded. I was sentenced to be 'Confined to lines' for three days. I tried to send my father a telegram advising him of this mischance so that he could cancel his visit, but somehow my message went astray and after the Church parade on Sunday the whole corps was inspected by my father, who was accompanied by Professor Lindemann. My father was led around by the General Officer Commanding Salisbury Plain, and when the inspecting party passed me the General's ADC said: 'The General would be glad if you would come to luncheon with your father.' As soon as parade was dismissed I hastened off to the Orderly Room, marched in and saluted the Adjutant, told him of this invitation and asked whether I might accept in spite of my being 'Confined to lines'. To my vast surprise he replied 'No'. I asked him how I could send a message to the General explaining my inability to come and he replied: 'I'll take care of that.' After luncheon my father and the 'Prof', who had driven nearly a hundred miles to see me, were allowed to visit me in camp and for more than an hour we strolled up and down the lines.

It was a lovely summer day, but the Professor, as usual, was wearing an overcoat, a bowler hat and carried an umbrella. I can't remember what we talked about, but my father thought it very funny and submitted himself, as I did, with good grace to the requirements of the military.

One was always glad when older friends proposed to come down to Eton and take one out to luncheon. One day Victor Cazalet, who was a Member of Parliament and who was a friend of my family's, said he would come down and take me to luncheon with the Provost, Dr M. R. James, the famous writer of eerie ghost stories. I had never met Dr James and was much excited by this invitation. Victor came and collected me at my house and led me across to the Provost's house. At the door Victor and a friend of his, whom I did not then know, were admitted; but I was told that I was not expected by the Provost. I returned to my house too late for boys' dinner and went down to Rowlands (the 'sock-shop' as Eton called what other schools call the 'tuck-shop') to get a sandwich. After luncheon Victor turned up in my rooms, apologised for the misunderstanding. He had brought P. G. Wodehouse with him. I had eight or nine copies of P. G. Wodehouse's books which had been successively given to me by the Prof, and I asked him to sign them. This he did, with great good will. They must be extremely valuable today: but alas, they have disappeared in the interval of the years.

I won only a single prize at Eton. There was a prize called the 'Junior Loder Prize', which was given for elocution. I happened to notice that my godfather, Lord Birkenhead, was coming down to judge it. I bethought me of Dr Alington's quatrain about 'push and pull'. I entered my name for the contest. Our main task was to declaim the celebrated passage from Ruskin which begins:

That which seems to be wealth may in verity be only the gilded index of far-reaching ruin; a wrecker's handful of coin gleaned from the beach to which he has beguiled an argosy; a camp-follower's bundle of rags unwrapped from the breasts of goodly soldiers dead; the purchase-price of potter's fields, wherein shall be buried together the citizen and the stranger.

And therefore, the idea that directions can be given for the gaining of wealth, irrespectively of the consideration of its moral sources, or that any general and technical law of purchase and gain can be set down for national practice, is perhaps the most insolently futile of all that ever beguiled men through their vices. So far as I know, there is not in history record of anything so disgraceful to the human intellect as the modern idea that the commercial text, 'Buy in the cheapest market and sell in the dearest', represents, or under any circumstances could represent, an available principle of national economy. Buy in the cheapest market? yes; but what made your market cheap? Charcoal may be cheap among your roof timbers after a fire, and bricks may be cheap in your streets after an earthquake; but fire and earthquake may not therefore be national benefits. Sell in the dearest? yes, truly; but what made your market dear? You sold your bread well to-day; was it to a dying man who gave his last coin for it, and will never need bread more, or to a rich man who to-morrow will buy your farm over your head; or to a soldier on his way to pillage the bank in which you have put your fortune?

I imparted my project to my father, supposing that he would be delighted that I was developing a more serious attitude towards my schooling. He was infuriated at the passage which the authorities had selected from Ruskin, pointing out that he himself was a Free Trader and this was a monstrous piece of Protectionist propaganda. He even suggested that it was rather bad taste for me to take advantage of my Godfather's visit in order to pick up a prize. I refused to allow myself to be discouraged. After all I had learnt the passage and thought that I could recite it very well; and its declamation, as I pointed out to my father, certainly in no way committed me to the views which it contained. In the event F.E. did not come and I shared the prize with three other boys. It must have been a very handsome prize, for I still have on my shelves finely-bound volumes of Shelley, Keats and Adam Lindsay Gordon to commemorate my success.

PART III: 1928–30

AT THE end of the Winter half of 1928, I got my house colours. This was the only athletic trophy I ever gained. It happened in this way: I had become a member of our house football team. I played post on the side, that is I was supported by two side posts in the scrum with which each portion of the play began. It wasn't called a scrum at Eton, it was called a bully. I was thought good enough to play in this position as I was small and was quite adroit at discharging my main task, which was when the ball was thrown into the bully to get it between my feet and hold it there against the kicks, or slicks as they were called, of the other side. The reason why I was good at this was that in addition to wearing ordinary shin pads which were of a light structure, I had had built for me a pair of aluminium shin pads which I wore outside the traditional ones and inside my stockings. Therefore I did not mind anyone kicking my shins! I was only sensitive in the ankles.

The Captain of Games was Southby, of whom I have already written. The amount of colours awarded depended on how well the house-team did; if one's team only reached the ante-final, as it was called, only six or seven were distributed; if into the final, eight or nine. But if the team won, everyone had to get it, even including the twelfth man. I shall long remember the off-hand way in which, after the game was over, which we had won, and while we all ambled in dog-tired, Southby took off his cap and flung it towards me. Fortunately I caught it.

This gaining of colours by me was I think the only regret at M'Tutors that night. It was nearly the end of the half but I hurried out next day to buy all the regalia that accompanied my house colours. There was a cap, there were stockings, there was an enormous woollen scarf, and a couple of shirts, probably amounting in all to £10 or £12. The colours were not particularly pretty. If I remember rightly, black, orange and magenta. However, I was very proud to have them, and particularly to wear them for a few days because of the displeasure which I knew this was causing to those boys in the house and school with whom I was unpopular. I was to have, as it turned out, very little opportunity of flaunting these feathers.

Three or four days later we broke up for the Christmas holidays. I joined my family at Chartwell. Early in the New Year I was told that the Prof was telephoning from Oxford and wished to speak to me. I went to the telephone with an apprehensive heart: I had recently passed my school certificate with sufficient credits to allow me to be admitted to Oxford, but I had a guilty conscience about the way I had managed to do this.

During the previous holidays before I took the exam my cousin Johnny, who was at Harrow, told me that he had failed the year before in the School Certificate, and that he would be doing the examination at Harrow at the same time that I would have to do it at Eton. We knew that the same papers were set for all entrances to Oxford. I wondered whether the academic authorities would have the good sense to synchronise the papers that were being set, and suggested to Johnny that we should exchange the timetables of the papers, and that if any failed to synchronise, we should, on a reciprocal basis, telephone to each other the questions which should by chance be submitted to either one of us ahead of the other. Sure enough, when the time came we found that there were one or two papers which were set in the morning at Harrow and in the afternoon at Eton, and vice-versa. I do not think that either of us obtained much advantage by the folly of the examiners, or by our somewhat illicit enterprise.

I remember Johnny telephoning me about twelve o'clock one day with a list of History questions. With two friends, who were in on this deal, I spent two hours in the school library looking up all the relevant facts and dates. Strangely enough I didn't do particularly well in this paper. I have always wondered since whether it was tantamount to cheating. I don't think so. If the authorities were so stupid as to publish the papers at Harrow some hours before they published them at Eton, it would surely have been negligent on our part to omit taking advantage of this. We would have been as foolish as the examiners. And it cannot be a part of education to encourage the pupils to be foolish.

All these recollections raced through my mind as I went to the telephone. Like so many of one's apprehensions in life, they proved unfounded. The Prof was merely ringing up rather excitedly to say that an extra place was available at the House – as Christ Church is familiarly known – for the January term; and if I could let him know straight away, I could be admitted forthwith. I said I would ring him back. I asked my father, who was overjoyed. I called the Prof back and immediately started making my arrangements.

The very next day I drove over with my sister Diana to Eton to collect all my goods and belongings. I found some method of disposing of the tawdry colours I had gained only ten days before, drove back to Chartwell and set about, with my mother's help, equipping myself for my new life. It was a thrilling moment.

Prof Lindemann had always been very kind to me while I was at Eton. He once came over from Oxford and picked me up in his Mercedes-Benz and took me to the cricket match between Eton and Winchester. We did not take much notice of the cricket – lawn tennis was the Prof's preferred game. We picnicked on the downs and there for the first time in my life I encountered that remarkable personality, Nancy Astor, who was taking one or two of her prolific family of sons out for the day. I was struck by her vivacity and still more by the copious supply of toast sandwiches which she offered me and which, I am bound to admit, were superior to those the Prof, who was a vegetarian, produced. I was to have many more encounters with Nancy Astor, always of a lively nature.

The Prof was rather a lonely man and he made a point of being very kind to children. I remember my Aunt Goonie, who often used to spend Christmas with us at Chartwell, as did the Prof, once said to a friend: 'There is something sinister about the Prof.' 'Oh really, why?' 'He gives the children presents,' my aunt hissed. Now this seemed to me a most amiable side of the Prof's character. I think my Aunt Goonie thought he must be a spy or something of that sort.

I went up to Oxford a good deal younger than people usually do. I was only seventeen and three-quarters when I arrived there for the January term. I went up some years later than my friend-to-be Evelyn Waugh did, in what he in his memoirs called a 'by-term'. I did not find this as inconvenient as he did. I wanted to get on in life as quickly as I could. I hadn't enjoyed or profited from Eton very much; I was keen to get to Oxford. I had not been a popular boy at Eton but I had made some friends; strangely enough, most of these went different ways and I was destined to see little of them in later years. I rather had a taste for friends older than myself – I enjoyed picking their brains. This was not easy at Eton where friendships, as I have shown, between younger and older boys were discouraged. At Oxford the age difference, of course, mattered little. At Eton I had already made friends, though rather from a distance because of the age gap, with Freddie Furneaux, Basil Dufferin, and Seymour Berry. They were all two or three years older than me and they had naturally preceded me to Oxford, but as I went there so exceptionally young they were still there when I arrived. They formed the nucleus of the many enduring friendships that I was to make at Oxford.

Freddie and Seymour were like myself at Christ Church.

Diana and RSC with some of the Mitford family: age 16. *l. to r.:*
Ralph Jarvis, Unity Mitford, Jessica Mitford, Diana Mitford,
Diana Churchill, Tom Mitford, RSC, Lady Redesdale

Amateur theatricals: *c.* 1928

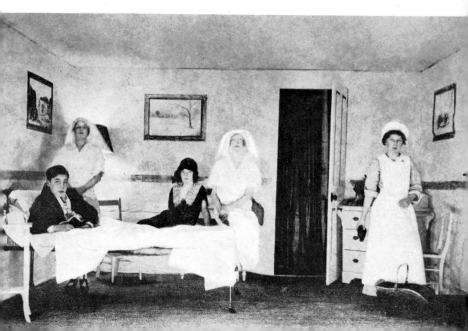

RSC: age 18

Basil, I think, was at Balliol. They seemed the most glittering and attractive people in what Freddie was pleased to call derisively 'the smart bunch'. All my life I have tended to make friends with people older than myself. I would counsel all other young men to do the same. One should seek to consort with one's intellectual peers or superiors, not with one's intellectual inferiors. On the other hand, as you approach middle age, it is a good thing to make friends with younger people. It is stimulating and invigorating and an insurance against a possibly lonely old age if you should happen to survive for an excessive period.

Freddie's father, the famous F.E. Smith, was my godfather and my father was Freddie's godfather. There was therefore naturally an assured basis of friendship here. F.E., though somewhat in his decline but still fascinating and wonderful to the eyes of youth, had a delightful house in Charlton, little more than twenty miles from Oxford. Thither we were all apt to repair on Saturdays and Sundays; tennis, golf, riding, swimming were the order of the day and in the evening anything up to sixteen people, mostly undergraduates, would be crammed into the small, panelled dining room.

It was F.E.'s habit to prompt us all to make after-dinner speeches upon which he would make caustic comments. The atmosphere was gay and witty, and I seemed to be moving into an enchanted world: an expansion of that which I had known in my boyhood at Chartwell but which I was now old enough to savour with full relish. I remember one evening, only a few months before F.E. died, when he sat morosely through dinner. Basil had just become engaged to the great heiress, Miss Maureen Guinness. F.E. took no part in the conversation but there was a lot of merry bad taste chatter promoted by Basil in a jocular vein as to what sort of presents he expected from all of us. This seemed to upset F.E. – perhaps he was thinking it would have been better if his own son had contracted so important an alliance. But he suddenly roused

E

himself and said: 'My dear Basil, I don't think you have much to concern yourself about. It seems to me that in this forthcoming union everything is arranged on one side or the other. You have a prospective father-in-law who is as rich as Croesus and whose generosity is unbridled. He owns a yacht the size of the *Berengaria*. I much underrate your ingenuity if I think you incapable of tapping those lavish resources.' This was said quite angrily and we all felt abashed. For two or three minutes no more was said until I think it was Frank Pakenham (now the Earl of Longford) produced a new topic of conversation.

At Oxford I continued to admire Freddie's fine memory and noble command of language. It was he who encouraged me to learn by heart Lecky's famous passage on prostitution from his *History of European Morals*. Despite a failing memory, I am glad to say I can still recite it today:

Under these circumstances there has arisen in society a figure which is the most mournful and in some respects the most awful upon which the eye of the moralist can dwell. That unhappy being, whose very name it is a shame to mention, who counterfeits with a cold heart the transports in affection and submits her body as a passive instrument of lust; who is scorned and insulted as the vilest of her sex and doomed for the most part to disease and abject misery and an early death, appears in every age as the perpetual symbol of the degradation and the sinfulness of man. Herself the supreme type of vice, she is ultimately the most efficient guardian of virtue. But for her, the unchallenged purity of countless happy homes would have been polluted; and not a few, who in the pride of their untempted chastity, think of her with an indignant shudder would have known the agony of remorse and of despair. On that one degraded and ignoble form are concentrated the passions that might have filled the world with shame. She remains while creeds and civilisations rise and fall the eternal priestess of humanity blasted for the sins of people.

It was by committing to memory such purple passages and others from Macaulay and Gibbon, and still others – less purple – from Keats, Shelley and Wordsworth that I early acquired a love for the English language. Although I have still not mastered it with exactitude it has been to me a perennial delight both in the spoken and the written word.

Many years later, during the Second World War, Freddie was visiting on behalf of the Political Warfare Executive the military sub-mission which I commanded in Croatia. While there he quoted some exquisite lines. They went as follows:

> Your beauty long ago is dust
> And dust your lovely hair,
> The ribbon and the scented robe
> That once you used to wear.
> You flung it round Caraxus
> And held him to your heart;
> That night you spent in rapture
> Till morning bade you part.
> But still in Sappho's flawless ode,
> Is your beloved name
> And lives for ever in a song,
> Oblivion cannot claim.
> So men must love you Dorica
> Whilst Naucratis shall be
> And ships shall stir the long lagoons
> Where Nilus meets the sea.

I asked Freddie to write this down for me; he did. I asked him for the source of it and he wrote contemptuously at the bottom in his fine handwriting, 'By Potts!' Freddie is very shy and I am convinced that he was responsible himself both for the passage about Henry VIII which he declaimed at Eton and for the poem about Dorica.

Incidentally, in none of the recorded and accepted odes of Sappho is Dorica's name mentioned. This seems to confirm my view that it was a gifted work of Freddie's imagination.

Strangely enough, Freddie with his own somewhat florid taste in literature, invented or exaggerated a story about myself falling into the same paths of error. He used to tell, and for all I know still does, a story of how the learned dons who were called upon to read my examination papers in history at Oxford went through them carefully looking for some statement of fact or recordings of some date for which they could award me a mark; but were regaled instead with this passage on Louis Quatorze: 'This Monarch was disfigured by all the vices that might have disgraced an Eastern potentate, swigging his wine and dandling his concubines while France mouldered into ruin.' It is a favourite story of Freddie's, and I am in no position to deny it.

In those days there was still a lot of social intercourse between undergraduates and dons. Some of the cleverest and wittiest of the dons and professors delighted in picking out those who they thought were the most promising undergraduates and inviting them to luncheon parties. We undergraduates used to give reciprocal luncheon parties in our rooms. So I would give four or five luncheons each term and was invited at least three or four times a week to similar festivities and potations by dons and by my fellow-undergraduates. The dons and professors who patronised me and entertained me and whom I entertained in return and whom I met at other luncheons were, of course, Prof Lindemann, my father's old friend, who lived in Meadow Buildings in the House, Maurice Bowra, not then knighted and only Dean of Wadham, Lord David Cecil, 'Sligger' Urquhart of Balliol, Roy Harrod of the House and I think John Sparrow, already a Fellow of All Souls. We were all rather cliquey on the undergraduate side; our luncheons were usually given by Freddie, Basil, Seymour and myself.

The luncheons followed a similar pattern. We would assemble at 1 o'clock and drink sherry. We sat down at 1.15; the first course was nearly always lobster Newburg, thereafter some meat dish, vegetables and some over-ornamented confection as a pudding. All of this came from the college kitchens and was really extremely inexpensive. We usually drank a hock with the meal and lots of port afterwards. The luncheons rarely broke up before 4 or even 4.30. It was always stimulating

68

and exhilarating and an education in itself. It was far less laborious than getting up early in the morning and going to lectures. At the luncheons one met the clever witty dons on level terms and learnt a great deal which was later to prove serviceable in the battle of life.

My father had caused me to be taught to ride but I was far from an expert horseman. I had enjoyed it and had hunted a little, but I did not tremendously care for it, not at any rate to the extent of being prepared to increase my growing over-drafts and my general indebtedness. An American friend of mine, Boy Scheftel, however, suggested that I should ride in a local point-to-point; he said he would pay the necessary fiver to hire a competent hack that would safely carry me around the course.

I found it impossible to resist the challenge. I came a nasty purler at the second fence, first time round, and the horse escaped and was rescued by some of the bystanders. I collected myself; I was only winded but had incurred a few scratches which caused quite a loss of blood. I plodded my way back more than half a mile across the countryside. Three or four of my friends, led by Freddie, came to meet me with concerned looks on their faces. But when I waved at them and told them that I was all right, Freddie in his sardonic way said: 'Randolph as usual: "Bloody but unbowed".'

At Oxford I had considerably renewed and fortified my long-standing friendship with my cousin Johnny Churchill. He had arrived some months before me at Oxford from Harrow. He was installed in some rather agreeable rooms in Pembroke, Dr Johnson's old college. I found him when I arrived and called on him, lying on a high platform near his ceiling, painting murals. He apparently did not come down for three days but had his food and drink and necessaries passed up to him.

Johnny cut a considerable figure at Oxford in various unusual ways. He was a fine swimmer and diver and a prodigious acrobat. I remember him on some occasion of high festivity when we were all attired in white ties and the candle-lit board had been laid, taking a running dive before dinner, and diving headfirst across the table doing a brisk somersault and landing unscathed upon his feet. We all enjoyed this very much.

When I was ten or eleven, and my older sister Diana was twelve or thirteen, my mother had spent a lot of money and taken a lot of trouble to teach us to play golf. Neither of us proved adept at this game or indeed at any other game. However when I went to Oxford I found that most of my friends played golf and so I tried to join in. I had two rather curious successes. A group of my friends bet me that I could not drive a golf ball out of Peckwater Quad. I was allowed three shots. I stationed myself with my back to the House library and teed up my ball with a wooden tee as high as possible in front of the library steps. I selected a mashie niblick for the shot as it was important to clear the three-storey façade which is only, I imagine, thirty or forty yards away. My first shot soared triumphantly out of Peckwater and I collected my bet. I never enquired what happened to the ball; nor did the authorities.

There were two very fine American golfers up at Oxford at that time, Charles and Bobby Sweeney. Bobby Sweeney was a great friend of mine and perhaps the better golfer of the two. He sought to encourage me to play golf and challenged me to a match. He offered me every imaginable number of strokes. I was shrewd enough to realize that as I often took nine or ten or eleven strokes over a hole, these would be inutile. Accordingly I insisted on 'bisques'. These were strokes that you could take at any hole you wished and were not pre-ordained hole by hole as is the case when you take strokes. I talked Bobby into offering me no fewer than thirty-two bisques. I calculated that on this basis I could even beat Bobby Jones, who was the Emperor of golf at this time. My calculation was that to win an eighteen-hole match I had only to win ten holes and that therefore I could afford to take any hole which only required three bisques. This proved to be right. When I did a hole in thirteen or fourteen I naturally did not take any bisques. I just gave up: but I accumulated a sufficient lead and was declared the winner before a fascinated audience of our friends by about the fifteenth hole. No such handsome offer has ever been made to me since. And so I retired from outdoor sport and took to indoor sports instead.

In May 1929 the Baldwin Government was defeated and the second minority Labour Government came into office. My father accordingly ceased to be Chancellor of the Exchequer though he still held his safe seat at Epping (now Woodford). My father determined to make a considerable voyage across Canada and the United States and to take with him my Uncle Jack, his son Johnny and myself. At the beginning of August we all embarked on the Canadian Pacific steamer the *Empress of Australia* and sailed for Quebec.

This was one of the very few periods of my life when I kept a diary; a few extracts may give some idea of our voyage and also of my outlook on life at the age of eighteen. I had been at Oxford for two terms. It was of course with immense excitement that Johnny and I set out on this adventure. Johnny was two years older than me and also an undergraduate at Oxford, at Pembroke.

Monday: August 5

Dr Johnson once said 'Being on a ship is like being in prison with the extra chance of being drowned'. In these days it would be more accurate to substitute sick for drowned, but in spite of the spacious accommodation there is much truth in the statement. I certainly can never remember a weekend which has passed so slowly. Writing of prison reminds me that in the course of a discussion between Papa & Amery on the subject of their school-life at Harrow, Papa said 'I have always had the greatest sympathy for convicts, and when Home Secretary always strove to reduce their sentences as I myself have undergone eleven years of penal servitude in the private and public schools of Britain!'

71

Twenty-One Years

Tuesday: August 6

. . . It must mournfully be admitted that the vast majority of one's fellow-men and women are dull, graceless, unattractive, gauche and boorish, and yet if one knew them probably very charming. Any way to themselves they are supremely important and no doubt serve some useful function. But the sight of them makes me sigh for the company of my friends . . .

On reading this I have a fervent hope that something of interest will soon happen. She who reads this diary will certainly have an uphill fight till we reach firm land once more.

Wednesday: August 7

Absolutely nothing today. Usual water-polo. In the evening a concert. Bad. Papa had to preside. Made quite a good speech. Met attractive Canadian girl. Hope tomorrow to see an iceberg. Very sleepy. Johnny anxious for sleep. Good night. Turn light out. PS. Papa called the company at dinner several times to bear record that soon there would be grave trouble in Egypt. He seemed very upset about this, but some 1865 brandy cheered him up.

Quebec. Friday: August 9

Just 12 pm and within less than a week of starting from Westerham, the birth-place of Wolfe, I am in bed thirteen stories above the scene where he met his death. This hotel is situated upon the very summit of the heights of Abraham. Below us is the St Lawrence bright with the lights of a hundred vessels.

Sunday: August 11

From our window we can see at night the Rothermere paper mills all lit up. Papa said apropos of them 'Fancy cutting down those beautiful trees we saw this afternoon to make pulp for those bloody newspapers, and calling it civilization'. Certainly the wonderful sights we saw this afternoon do induce in one a great reaction against the modern highly-developed existence.

Monday: August 12

We are certainly being entertained in this country in a most princely fashion. At 11.30 we drove to the station where we found drawn up a most palatial private car – the Mount Royal – some ninety feet in length. It is to be our headquarters for the next three weeks, and it certainly possesses every convenience and comfort. It comprises a dining room, a sitting room, three bedrooms, two bathrooms, four lavatories and kitchen and an observation platform at the back. We have our own cook and waiter who both live on the car. There are three or four fans in each room a powerful wireless set which plays in the sitting room and the dining room by the mere pressing of a button. One could not travel in more luxurious fashion. The car belongs to Mr Hall, the Vice-President of the Canadian Pacific Railway, and we can just hook it on to any train that happens to be passing and then stop wherever we like.

We arrived at Montreal at 6.30 having travelled about 180 miles from Quebec. We attended a dinner at the Mount Royal Club which included the fifty most prominent business men in Montreal which is a city with a population of considerably over a million. Mr Beatty the Chairman of the CPR presided and Papa made an extremely effective speech of about thirty-five minutes which was well-received. He spoke without notes and without preparation and proved what I have always believed that the effect on the actual audience is far greater if the delivery is absolutely spontaneous. Of course for a speech to read well long preparation and even notes are essential, but after all the influence the speech has on the audience is the primary consideration. I think Papa is gradually coming round to my point of view and is relying less and less upon notes. John Morley once said 'Three things matter in a speech – who says it, how he says it, and what he says, and of the three the last matters the least'. How true.

Montreal. Tuesday: August 13

In reading the Canadian papers I have noticed one particular trait. As a rule they are much like the English ones but they have a curious way of announcing deaths. Three forms I have noticed being 'Mr So & So joins the Majority'; 'Death calls for Mr So & So'; and most supremely exquisite of all – 'The death of Sir Edward Kemp adds one more to the roll of necrology of famous statesmen!'

Wednesday: August 14

This morning one of the ADCs took me for a spin in his speed-boat on the Ottawa river. It was most thrilling, and we went about thirty-five mph. Papa and Uncle Jack and Johnny and I then motored out to Kingsmere to lunch with McKenzie King. He lives in a sweet little house in lovely surroundings. He was most interesting and enlightening about Canada, and seemed to me a very thoughtful and purposeful man. We stayed there till about five and then returned to Government House.

A large dinner of some thirty people tonight. Quite amusing. After dinner we danced. Blossom Forbes-Robertson (who has married Willingdon's son – Freeman Thomas) is here. She is very attractive in fact almost beautiful . . .

Ottawa. Thursday: August 15

In the evening we dined with Sir Robert Borden, who was PM for nine years. About fifteen people including McKenzie King who I think is one of the most delightful men I have ever met. He was very kind to me, and took great trouble to be agreeable.

Friday: August 16

At seven this morning we arrived at Toronto, and at nine drove to the Lieutenant-Governor's house where we breakfasted. I had a slight fracas with a reporter at the station who wanted to know what was the first sound I heard on arriving at Toronto. This led to a rather rude paragraph in the evening paper making out that I had been discourteous to the Press. Papa very angry with me.

EP [*Prince of Wales*'] *Ranch, Alberta. Saturday: August 24*

I happened to say (after seeing the Calgary oilfields) that it was a depressing thing to see all these oil magnates pigging up a beautiful valley to make fortunes and then being quite incapable of spending their money, and went on to criticise their lack of culture. Instantly Papa flared up, 'Cultured people are merely the glittering scum which floats upon the deep river of production!' Damn good.

Banff. Tuesday: August 27

At three we reached Emerald Lake, a small lake of an exquisite shade of turquoise. On the side of it is a little bungalow encampment in which we are sleeping. In the afternoon Papa painted quite a good picture. I went in a little boat upon the lake and sunbathed. Later we rode. Uncle Jack setting out ahead of me met a bear six foot high, which fled.

Saturday: August 31

At twelve o'clock we set out on an expedition to the glacier. Papa came out looking magnificent. Jodhpur riding suit of khaki, his ten gallon hat, a malacca walking stick with gold knob, and riding a pure white horse. We rode up to the Lake of the Clouds and then on to the edge of the moraine where we had lunch at two o'clock. We then rode on after seeing two marmots very tame and peaceful about eighteen inches long. Arrived at the glacier. Papa, Johnny and I climbed all over it – Papa with especial vigour.

Monday: September 2

At 12.30 we started to participate in the opening ceremonies at the Exhibition at New Westminster about ten miles from here. We lunched off the most disgusting cold buffalo which was ushered in by the singing of 'Rule Britannia'. After lunch everyone made presentations to everyone else. The Queen of the May and her attendants were given medals (though why September is not a close season for May Queens I could not discover). Then various gents accepted trophies on behalf of other absent gents. Then we had singing first a soprano then a tenor. Once again 'Rule Britannia', followed by Papa's speech to the luncheon (about seven minutes).

We next went out to open the exhibition. More 'Rule Britannia' and presentations. Then Papa made another speech (about twenty minutes). Next we were told that Papa had got to 'face off' at a lacrosse match, but by this time we had had enough, and we escaped.

Vancouver. Wednesday: September 4

Yesterday morning we drove about thirty miles out of Vancouver to visit a lumber camp. First we saw two men cut down a gigantic tree about two hundred feet high in about half an hour. Before it fell they showed us exactly what trees it would hit and what it would miss, and when it fell they were right to the identical inch.

Then we saw what is known as a high-rigger. A man puts on a pair of steel spurs, and ties himself to the tree with a rope and then climbs up the tree at a great pace lopping off the branches as he goes. This tree was even higher than the previous one – about three hundred feet – and was intended to be used as a rest on which to fix pulleys, so that the other trees could be more easily handled. So when the man had got up to a hundred and eighty feet, he cut off the top of the tree, which fell with an awe-inspiring crash. But for Papa's admonition to the contrary, he would then have stood on his head on the stump one hundred and eighty feet in the air.

After he had come down I fitted on the spurs and the belt and rope and climbed a little way up a smaller tree. It was really quite easy, but I doubt if I could have manipulated an axe!

Victoria. Friday: September 6

Johnny and I started the day with a bathe. Then lunch at the Canadian Club. Papa received a rapturous reception – the best he has had. He made a different speech from his stock one, which was an almost perfect example of his oratorical powers. I had been told that I would not be required to speak, but a fatuous dean proposed the vote of thanks. He meandered on for more than a quarter of an hour. His humour was pathetic. 'I want,' he said, 'to ask Mr Churchill three questions – If he ever becomes Prime Minister will he make me Archbishop of Canterbury? Does he intend to go into business with Lord Birkenhead? Is he still a member of the bricklayers' union?' I immediately saw the opportunity to make a hit, and glanced down the table at Papa who nodded his assent; so as soon as the old dean sat down I arose to reply. They were all so bored by the dean that anything would have pleased them. Sensing the atmosphere I proceeded very mildly to twit the dean, and to answer the asinine questions as humorously as possible. I only spoke for about five minutes but I achieved the greatest success I have ever had. They all roared with laughter, and cheered lengthily when I sat down. Papa was delighted. It was not, I must admit, in any way a good speech or particularly amusing, but I had the good fortune just to catch hold of what was wanted . . .

In the afternoon we went and fished for salmon on the sea. Uncle Jack caught a ten pounder – no one else had a bite except myself. I hooked no less than three, but each time although I let them have their heads the hook on the spoon broke. It was most disappointing. However as Papa remarked 'Tis better to have hooked and lost, than never hooked at all.'. . .

11.45. The train is just leaving Seattle [USA]. I am lying on the top berth of our compartment. Papa is unpacking and swearing down below. We miss the Mount Royal . . . In order to preserve the chronology of this account, I think it would be well before giving my impressions of our arrival, to sum up briefly my reactions to Canada.

The most striking characteristic is the supreme loyalty manifested on all sides towards England and the Empire, coupled with an intense dislike of America. For the purposes of party politics the Liberals and Mackenzie King are made to appear as too friendly to America and disloyal to England, but this is not really so. Everywhere I have seen the most marked signs of genuine sympathy and affection for what they all term the 'Old Country'. Canadians wish to see a firmer attitude adopted by England towards the US. Even if the Liberals were to play up to the US too much they would inevitably be checked by the French Canadians who are the real strength of their party. They would never contemplate union with America as they wish to preserve their religious independence. They are really very Conservative, and it is chiefly the memory of Sir Wilfrid Laurier the great French-Canadian Liberal Prime Minister which keeps them with the Liberals.

The second thing that struck me was how much I felt at home. Although there is little culture here, and the Canadians are crude and possess all the usual traits of a young nation, the people are not blatant or vulgar. They have the same ideals and sentiments as we do, and are very easy to make friends with. The fundamental point is this 'We are all part of the same show' and it is still possible to be proud of it despite Kipling. [This like many other of my youthful opinions was absurdly jejune; I am now a keen admirer of Kipling, his poetry and his prose.]

Thirdly they are developing with astonishing rapidity. As Papa has said in his speeches, while the trek to the West has been the work of the last twenty-five years the roll to the north will mark the next quarter of a century. The discovery that corn will grow right up to the Arctic circle opens new possibilities and territories, previously useless to man. It is too difficult to write in this train. I will continue this tomorrow.

. . . One small but significant fact is that there are no beggars in Canada. No one is destitute. All can earn a satisfactory living . . .

. . . We are now on the ship bound to Seattle, American soil and Prohibition. But we are well-equipped. My big flask is full of whiskey and the little one contains brandy. I have reserves of both in medicine bottles. It is almost certain that we shall have no trouble. Still if we do, Papa pays the fine, and I get the publicity. But we have a second line of reserves. We questioned the Chief of Police in Vancouver as to the best arrangements to be made and he said he would telephone and have some put on the train at Seattle. We asked him who would see to it. His reply shows how graft-stricken the US is: 'The police'! He knows the Chief of Police at Seattle, and he will readily oblige. Of course it is the Federal Police who are really responsible for drink, but still one cannot conceive of a situation like that in England.

Seattle. Saturday: September 7

The Chief of the Customs came on board, also the British Vice-Consul. One would expect that if they take the trouble to inflict their personal company upon us they would waive all formalities. On the contrary they asked dozens of questions, and when they heard that we had some camera-plates, gave us to understand that ordinarily they would have been subjected to the closest scrutiny to discover if any of them were of an obscene nature, but that they would dispense with this as a great favour. 'How many cigars?' was one of their questions. As Papa had a diplomatic visa and a letter from Dawes asking the Customs to give us every consideration, this seemed to me very remarkable. However all went well and I landed with my two flasks, and with my attaché-case with two medicine bottles of whiskey and brandy. The Chief of the Customs accompanied us to the hotel where we were entertained by the Manager, who provided some quite good beer. The prohibition officer would not have any himself, but did not at all object. He explained that the Government took little interest in the ultimate consumer, but concentrated its warfare on the bootlegger – which is rather lucky for us as the ultimate consumer is the only person in whom we really are interested.

. . . I forgot to mention an amusing incident at Seattle, which shows how much more pushing and assertive the Press are than in England. An attractive young lady from some paper greeted me on the quay with the words 'Do we see you now or on the train?' Notice the '*Do*'. It is a foregone conclusion that they have an interview. I answered rather tartly 'I'm not sure you see us at all'. But she turned up at the train and interviewed Papa for about ten minutes. He was rather captivated I am afraid, and put up with it. Then she turned on me and asked me if I was going to marry an American wife. I merely replied that I did not intend to reveal my matrimonial plans at present, and walked away. The Press should I think be made to realise that an interview is a favour and not an obligation. (I wonder if Seymour would agree.)

En route to San Francisco. Sunday: September 8

We got away from Grant's Pass about eight, and at half past eleven reached Eureka. From time to time on the way we passed great groves of Redwood trees. These are about ten foot in diameter, about two hundred and fifty to three hundred feet high, and anything between fifteen hundred and five thousand years old. They were a most lovely sight, like the great pillars of a cathedral. One tree attained a height of two hundred and eighty-seven feet before it had a branch.

At Eureka we met a young man who has just gone down from the House called Watson. He is in the Consulate at San Francisco, and is motoring south with us to reduce the squash in the one car. We also met the Captain of the British cruiser *Colombo*. He got the VC for the sinking of the Russian battleships at Kronstadt in 1919.

We motored another twenty miles before lunch, making one hundred and twenty in all. After lunch we bathed, 'au naturel' in a deliciously warm stream, and then inspected the largest tree in California – three-hundred and eighty feet high. We met several naval officers at the tree, and we all joined hands and pressing ourselves against the tree and stretching as far as we could made a circle round the tree. We then numbered smartly from the left, and found it took fourteen of us! It must have been more than twenty feet thick.

En route to San Francisco. Monday: September 9

We started about ten am and after about one hundred miles arrived at a Frenchman's house. I can't recall his name, but he makes the wine which is used for sacramental purposes. He had a charming daughter who is married to a French Count. We had a most delicious lunch and drank some of the sacramental wine, which was very good – a sort of white wine. He had also some very good 1825 brandy. In the garden there were the most exquisite butterflies and humming birds.

After lunch we visited his wine store. Enormous barrels were every-where. He has a stock of over a million gallons, and sells about two hundred thousand annually. He is only allowed to sell it to the priests but they pass it on to their friends. There are apparently five other 'wineries' like this; so Christ has come to the aid of Bacchus in a most wonderful way. They also sell unfermented grape-juice to individuals and then send men to ferment it, thus keeping the law, but circumventing prohibition.

San Francisco. Tuesday: September 10

I did not get up till about eleven this morning, and then it was too late to go into San Francisco, so I went round the garden. It is quite lovely and absolutely gigantic, and the flowers certainly belie the statement of M de la Tour of the sacramental wine who summed up California 'Fleurs sans odeur, femmes sans pudeur et hommes sans honneur'.

I then bathed in the most lovely swimming pool in the grounds here. Then lunch – just us four and Mrs Russel – Crocker's daughter. A most delightful woman and very well informed. Talked knowledgeably about stocks and shares, but I don't find this very attractive in a woman. Her husband is a stockbroker. The exchange opens here at six am. So as to synchronise with New York. Not my line at all.

In the evening Johnny and I attended a dinner-dance party at the big hotel in 'Frisco. Given for Patsy Tobin. Prohibition is a complete farce. We had cocktails in a private room upstairs, but dined in the ballroom. But champagne appeared in a large silver canister – plenty of it and very good. I met a very attractive married lady (about twenty-three) who is the image of Diane Bridgeman, only fair. I am going to ride with her at nine tomorrow and as it is already three am I must try and get a little beauty sleep.

San Simeon. Friday: September 13

A motley crowd of twenty-five guests are here. Mostly very inferior. Mrs Hearst who is quite too charming is here and consequently Marion Davies is not. The wife of Hearst's eldest son is here. He is a fat oaf, but she is exquisite. I suppose it was the money that got her. They ran away when they were both eighteen. During dinner I got a bloody old lawyer to lay the young Mrs Hearst and myself one hundred dollars to twenty against two identical cards turning up simultaneously when two packs are gone through together. It is exactly an even chance and we won eighty dollars each! Big ramp!!

Saturday: September 14

The most deliciously warm weather I have ever known greeted me on arising about ten. I have only had time to examine one-twentieth of the extraordinary products of William Randolph Hearst's fantasies and whims. The outside of the house is of white stone, and towers up to two Moorish turrets. The effect is like the façade of a great cathedral. Unfortunately an enormous wooden roof of great antiquity has been placed below the towers and though it is of unexampled beauty it does not match the rest. Inside the chief interest lies in an enormous room double cube in shape, and about one hundred and fifty feet long. It has a magnificent oak roof, and at night is lit by four hundred electric light bulbs. There is also a dining room of equal size – in the baronial fashion. These are the only two rooms I have seen so far, but upstairs there is a library just as remarkable. I will inspect it tomorrow.

The house stands on the top of a hill, about three miles from the sea, and two thousand feet above it. The ranch – for so it is termed in false modesty – comprises three hundred square miles, stretching along thirty-five miles of sea. The house is absolutely chock full of works of art obtained from Europe. They are insured for sixteen million dollars – ie three and a half million sterling. Hearst is reputed to possess an income of twenty million dollars!

Blenheim

Chartwell

(*above*) RSC: Canada
c. 1930

RSC

The house and grounds are by no means completed, though nine years have passed since it was started. Everywhere are workmen, motor lorries, pneumatic drills. The bathing pool has already been demolished twice, and now is entirely lined with black and white marble. The two or three acres surrounding it are in process of being paved in marble too.

In the garden, on one of the dozen or so terraces there is a full-sized cinematograph apparatus. Each night so far we have had talking films. One of the subsidiary houses possesses the most divine overhanging moorish windows that can be imagined. Monasteries, palaces and castles throughout Europe have been and still are being ransacked for gems of one kind and another . . .

San Simeon. Monday: September 16

Old Mrs Hearst tonight made a most wonderful remark which shows that even the nicest people out here suffer from megalomania and over-weening pride. Speaking of Arthur Brisbane – Hearst's right-hand man who writes syndicated leaders for all the yellow press, she said 'The relationship between Voltaire and Frederick the Great is not unlike that between Brisbane and Mr Hearst.'

Wednesday: September 18

At 12.30 we attended a lunch given at Hollywood in the Metro-Goldwyn-Mayer studios, by Mr Mayer and Hearst. He has a very large financial interest in this company. There were about two hundred people at the lunch – mostly film stars and producers. We met Marion Davies – Collen Moore – Anita Page – Joan Crawford – Douglas Fairbanks junior – Ramon Novarro, and many others of whom I had not heard. I thought Marion Davies was the most attractive. After lunch during which an orchestra of about twenty played continuously, various stars appeared on a stage at the far end of the room and performed. It really was astounding. They had a beauty chorus of twenty-five all of them infinitely more attractive than the best in London. A man sang who is paid a thousand pounds a night in New York and there were various other turns of exceptionally high order.

Then general speeches were made. Hearst very good and helpful, and much more friendly to England than expected. Then Papa spoke, and at the end of his speech, a man proposing a vote of thanks said 'I can only say that I would like to hear it again, and I dare say Mr Churchill could bear a little of it'! Whereupon through a hole in the roof came the speech again – absolutely perfect in tone and volume, and as clear as when he spoke himself!

Throughout lunch we were photographed by hordes of men and after lunch Papa, Hearst and Mayer had a talking film made of them. We then visited various studios and watched them 'shoot the scenes'. It was most absorbing. They have about six cameras so as to get it from every angle . . . The Metro-Goldwyn-Mayer have forty thousand persons on their pay roll which amounts to seventeen million dollars annually!

Santa Barbara. Thursday: September 19

Hearst has certainly been greatly won over by Papa. Not only did he make his very helpful speech yesterday, but today it is all featured in the Los Angeles *Examiner*. This morning he rang up to know how soon we were returning to Los Angeles, and seemed delighted when we said we would come to lunch tomorrow. One thing particularly amused me in his speech. He said that Papa had been anxious that there should not be too much speaking 'like the man who did not take his wife abroad as he was going for pleasure'. Considering that he had just left Mrs Hearst and was in Los Angeles with his mistress – Marion Davies – it seemed to me rather good value! We make an early start tomorrow, so no more now.

Hollywood. Saturday: September 21

Yesterday we motored into Hollywood from Santa Barbara and lunched at the Montmartre Restaurant – the luncheon haunt of the cinema world. Hearst, Marion Davies, P. G. Wodehouse and daughter, Ogden Stuart (the American P.G.), Virginia Vallia and four or five others were there. P.G. was in great form, and it was delightful meeting him again – this time without his lion-hunter Victor.

After lunch we visited various studios and then went out to Marion's house to bathe. It is about seventeen miles from Los Angeles. It is a magnificent place looking on the sea, with a wonderful marble swimming bath of great length and very well heated – all provided by William Randolph. Marion had collected a dinner party of sixty for us. Jim and David Smith were there. The stars included Pola Negri, Charlie Chaplin, Harold Lloyd, Billie Dove and Diana Ellis. I failed to recognise either Charlie or Harold, since moustache and horn-rimmed spectacles were missing.

After dinner we danced and then Marion stimulated Charlie into doing some impersonations. He did Sarah Bernhardt and Lillian Gish, and then he did Napoleon, Uriah Heep, Henry Irving, John Barrymore as Hamlet and many others. He is absolutely superb and enchanted every one. He also did terribly complicated patter dancing as also did Marion. She is delightfully stimulating and must have danced and frolicked around for about one and a half hours after a hard day's work.

Papa and Charlie sat up till about three. Papa wants him to act the young Napoleon and has promised to write the Scenario.

Thursday: September 26

The last few days have written nothing, as we have invariably been to bed so late. I will briefly record what we have done. On Monday we attended a large lunch given by Page the banker. I made a short speech. Very bad, but quite a hit. Johnny and I dined alone and went to a theatre. Papa and Uncle Jack dined with McAdoo – only dry meal Papa has had.

On Tuesday we lunched with Charlie at his studio. He was too sweet for words. He showed us *Shoulder Arms* and also part of his new film – *City Lights*. In the evening Marion gave a party for the first night of the *Cock-Eyed World* – the worst film I have ever seen. But all the movie world were there. We saw Carpentier who is out here. Charlie was in our party, also Diana Ellis, Jim and his sister. A first night is a terrific event. About ten searchlights are erected in the streets, and as all the stars come in their remarks are broadcasted. After the film we returned to the Roosevelt Hotel and danced. At dinner sherry and champagne was served quite openly.

Wednesday: October 2

At ten thirty this morning we arrived at Chicago – reputed the most cosmopolitan town in the world. Its population of three millions includes more Poles than there are in Warsaw, more Jews than there are in Jerusalem, and it is also the third largest German city [in the world].

We were met by 'Bernie' Baruch, McClellan and Pease. Baruch is the greatest speculator there has ever been. He actually bought a seat on the New York Stock exchange costing one hundred thousand pounds solely in order to transact his own business. During the war he was Chairman of the War Industries Board, and came into considerable contact with Papa. He is a tall man about six foot five inches, of great dignity and with a magnificent carriage and personality. He is one of the leading Democrats. The other two, Pease and McClellan are our hosts here and are the leading business men of the town . . .

We travelled across the American Continent from Los Angeles to Chicago in the private railway car of Mr Charles M. Schwab of the Bethlehem Steel Corporation. On arrival in Chicago where we were shown round the stockyards, and attended a prize fight, we were escorted by Mr Bernard M. Baruch in another private car to New York where we stayed with him at the fine house he then occupied on Fifth Avenue. Mr Baruch was an old friend of my father's since the two of them had been in 1917 and 1918 respectively Chairman of the War Industries Board and Minister of Munitions. They co-operated together very well so as to avoid Allied competition for scarce materials, Baruch was very proud of the fact that he had made my father the copper king of the world. My father bought all the copper and apportioned it fairly to suit the needs of the Allies and Associated Powers.

Leaving Chicago in the train Baruch told us the fascinating story of how he had made his first fortune at the age of twenty-six. He and a group of associates had conducted a bear operation against a copper company which today forms part of the Anaconda Company. The operations were long, anxious and intense. The crux was to come the next day. But when he got home he found a message from his mother – who was a strict Orthodox Jewess – saying 'I hope you will observe the Day of Atonement'. So he rang his office and said, 'I shan't be coming to the office tomorrow, don't telephone. If the market rises more than five points we shall have to clear out, but don't consult me.'

My father listened breathless to this tale of high finance. He had just ceased to be Chancellor of the Exchequer; he listened to the story with mounting interest and at this moment in the story exclaimed with tremendous anguish: 'But Jehovah did not betray his servant?' 'No Sir,' said Baruch. 'The stock broke forty points. Of course if I'd been there we'd have taken our profit after ten points. As it was all I had to do the following morning was to get down there and take the shirts off their backs. I found myself at the age of twenty-six, having made seven hundred thousand dollars in a day.'

New York. Monday: October 7

Jim [Smith] took us to a speak-easy called 'Tony's'. It was the mildest place I have ever seen, and much more respectable than an English pub; – most of the people seemed to be drinking lemonade. We had a half-bottle of champagne – Lanson '21 quite good but costing eight dollars or about two and a half times as much as in London.

Friday: October 11

After the theatre Johnny and I separated ourselves from the others, and Jim having refused to come with us, we set off alone to inspect Harlem, about which there is so much talk. It was really very disappointing. We first went to the Cotton Club. It was quite difficult to get in, as we had no ladies with us. There was quite a good Cabaret of rather a sensual nature, but everyone there was most respectable. So we soon moved on to the 'Nest'. This was very hard to get into. However, after some money had changed hands we got inside and were made members. I gave Seymour's name! The proprietor was a most sinister man, but everything was very tame. There must have been much more going on behind scenes, as outwardly it was not unlike the 'Bat', apart from all the secrecy.

After our tour of America, it was necessary for Johnny and me to come home ahead of my father and Uncle Jack. I was going to be two days late for the opening of the Oxford term anyway. F.E. was on the same boat and I dined with him every night. Every night too we played bridge together. F.E. played for fairly high stakes and he carried me for much lower stakes. It is still in my mind whether F.E. or I was the worse bridge player. We were pitted almost invariably against two very rich middle-aged American ladies who almost invariably won.

It fell to F.E. to deliver the speech at the ship's concert and to make an appeal for funds for distressed mariners – always an embarrassing occasion which, I think, has now been abandoned. He spoke in his usual and impressive style and was somewhat disappointed by the collection at the end. This was just before the market broke. The following night, while we were at the bridge table, the chief steward approached one of our friends with a large waste-paper basket full of pound notes and dollar bills and said, 'Here are your winnings from the pool on the ship's run.' There was certainly seven or eight hundred pounds in the waste-paper basket. F.E., irritated by his losses at the bridge table and even more by the relative failure of his own appeal for the benefit of 'those in peril on the sea', turned to the ladies who together had won the pool and said, 'How much did you give to the appeal which I delivered last night?' They said courageously, 'We each gave twenty dollars.' 'Inadequate', quoth F.E. He put his hand into the waste-paper basket and handed what he had indiscriminately grabbed to the chief steward saying, 'Tell the purser to add this extra contribution from the two ladies who won the pool tonight'. The two ladies looked furious but did not dare to tackle F.E.

My father, who was F.E.'s greatest friend, had brought me up on all the famous anecdotes illustrating his wit, brilliance and arrogance. Without F.E.'s learning or his majestic command of language, I sought to emulate his style of polished repartee. It didn't work in my case. I did not have my godfather's shining abilities and could not aspire to his brilliant gift of repartee. Nor did I have his industry or fit myself for a profession to earn my living. I, therefore, took up the calling for which no credentials or examinations are required – journalism. This was to lead me to a chequered career – sometimes up and sometimes down, but in which I now think, at the age of 53, I am beginning to prevail. At the time I was twenty-one we were already moving into a softer world where rough talk was much discouraged and deprecated. However clever and facile I was, I lost friends and failed to influence people. But I boxed on, though in the process somewhat damaged fair prospects which were open to me. I shall tell about this much later.

Tuesday: November 18

Our six days on the *Berengaria* were one long laugh. Henry McGowan and F.E. were both very kind to us and in terrific form. Worthy [Sir Laming Worthington-Evans, former Secretary of State for War] was terribly bullied by F.E. Tom met me at Waterloo and motored to Chartwell with me for the night.

PART IV: 1930–2

IN THE summer of 1930 when I was supposed to be working very hard at Oxford for my history preliminary examination some of my friends suggested that we should go to the Derby. Four or five of us drove over; I knew nothing about horse racing and know little more today, but we had the newspapers with us and there was lively speculation about the race. On the way we passed a kennel advertising Blenheim spaniels for sale. I had noticed that there was a horse called Blenheim running in the race. I thought this was an omen. When we arrived at the course, the first person I saw was my first cousin once removed, the Duke of Marlborough. I considered this a further omen. At this time I had no account with a bookmaker so I went to the rails and put a pound each way on Blenheim. My friends and I then mounted to the private boxes in the stands to which we thought we could obtain access through the good-will of some of our friends. The first person I encountered was my god-father, Lord Birkenhead. 'Ah, my dear boy,' he said, 'I am so gratified to notice that you are able to drag yourself away from your studies at Oxford for this important occasion. Come into this box.' He led me in and there was my father. He did not seem best pleased.

I was suitably attired in morning coat and top hat but of course I had no binoculars. But anyway, glasses or no glasses, I was ill-equipped to understand the race, though I had memorised the colours that Blenheim was to carry – the chocolate and green of the Aga Khan. As the horses neared the winning post I said excitedly: 'Blenheim is going to win, Blenheim is going to win.' The racing narks in the box said, 'Bloody fool,

Rastoum, Rastoum all the way'. (Rastoum Pasha was the preferred horse in the Aga Khan's stable and had started favourite at 9–4: it ran eleventh). I felt terribly ignorant and abashed, but when the numbers went up Blenheim was the winner – at eighteen to one. I seem to remember that by investing ready cash on the rails I had obtained rather longer odds. I had another successful bet, and left the course with forty or fifty pounds in my pocket – a rare occurrence.

One day my friends and I heard that some enterprising and publicity-seeking undergraduates had formed an Oxford University Balloon Club and that the prime mover of the venture was the son of the famous playwright Nigel Playfair. It was announced that a famous American actress, Miss Tallulah Bankhead, was coming down and would make the first ascent in the new club's balloon, so up we went to the local airport. But the affair had been ill-organised and turned out to be a fiasco. There were not enough gas cylinders to inflate the balloon and Miss Bankhead went back to Oxford with young Mr Playfair. Bobby Sweeney drove me back in his open two-seater blue Chrysler (I did not have a car of my own at the time). We overtook them in the streets of Oxford, waved wildly at them, announced our identities and invited them to join us in my rooms in the House. They agreed.

So Bobby and I repaired there and laid on some suitable refreshment for our distinguished guest, though we didn't really think that she would turn up. But turn up she did, and I seemed to hit it off well with her. She certainly hit it off very well with me. With the self-confidence of youth I said: 'When I come up to London one day soon, could I take you out to supper, Miss Bankhead?' And she said: 'Certainly. I am not acting at the moment so come round and have a drink at my house in Farm Street.' This invitation I joyfully accepted.

So a few days later, in high excitement, I went to London and at about six o'clock called upon Miss Bankhead at her house. Many people were there and it was difficult to establish any intimate contact with her. Contact seemed desirable on the grounds of her beauty and her glamour. So I said, 'Could I take you out to dinner?' She said, 'No, I am afraid I am booked up for that; but if you would like to come back about eleven you can take me to a bottle party'. I readily accepted the suggestion.

I returned to Seamore Place, the house of Sir William Berry. His son, Seymour, had very kindly told me that I could spend the night there. As I did not at that time belong to a London club, I made some enquiries over the telephone of some of my older friends to discover what a bottle party was and what the obligations were. I had never heard of this institution before. I was told that you must take a bottle. This worried me a great deal. The only restaurant I knew was the Maison Basque in Dover Street. I took a taxi and went there and asked for a bottle of whisky or champagne. But even the promise of ready cash (in this enterprise money was no object) was of no avail. They said that they did not have an off-licence and they could not help me in the matter. Disconsolately I returned for dinner to Seamore Place. I dined alone. I did not have the courage to ask the butler to help me in the matter, and after dinner was over I went upstairs, had a bath and changed into my dinner jacket and then came down to the dining room where there was a large decanter of whisky. I meditated borrowing the decanter, and I then thought that perhaps it might get lost at a bottle party. So I carried it reverently upstairs to my bathroom, which was in fact Seymour's when he was in London, and opened one of the numerous bottles of hair oil which he kept there and poured it down the sink. I then had to wash it copiously and repeatedly. I filled it five or six times with water and shook it and threw the water out. After this lengthy process, during all of which time I was terrified of being interrupted, I was in a keen state of apprehension. However, the bottle, cleansed of the revolting hair oil, I then filled it with the whisky from the decanter. It was not a large hair-oil bottle, and probably only took half of the decanter. I then took the depleted decanter downstairs, replaced it on the sideboard in the dining room, returned upstairs, completed my toilet and emerged to wait upon Miss Bankhead.

When I arrived at Farm Street fully equipped I was glad to find Miss Bankhead disencumbered from the noisy throng who had surrounded her earlier in the evening. In a husky voice she said, 'Darling, let's go'. I got a taxi and we drove off to somewhere in Regent's Park. I noticed that she had not brought a bottle, but was much ashamed of my own miserable stolen little contribution which I think I concealed from her. On arrival there was a lot of shouting and noisy music but in the hall which was I think that of a largish flat there was a table on which there were many bottles. When I thought no one was looking I surreptitiously took the bottle out of my pocket and placed it in the back of the row. It later transpired that my anxieties had been unnecessary – half the guests came without bottles.

I did not know anyone at the party and Miss Bankhead was soon absorbed, engulfed, and effectively surrounded. I had naïvely supposed that she was my girl for the night and even had higher aspirations. I never got near her again. But as I knew no one at this noisy masquerade I returned at an early hour to Seamore Place to lick my wounds. It was an admirable lesson. When I returned to Oxford I owned up to Seymour about my theft of his father's whisky and offered to replace it. Seymour made light of the whole affair and seemed happy to have been indirectly involved in it.

It was not for three or four years that I had the opportunity of meeting Miss Bankhead again – but that is another story which forms no part of my very early life.

One day when I was at Oxford Brendan Bracken arrived from London with Charlie Baillie-Hamilton and his beautiful exotic-looking wife Wanda. They were on their way down to Bath which Charlie represented in Parliament. Brendan and

Charlie said, 'Come along Randolph and we will all make speeches down there'. I explained that I would find it difficult to get leave but Brendan, who now had much more self-assurance, said, 'Don't bother about that, I'll fix everything'. So down we drove to Bath where there was a loud-speaker van and we all made speeches in the streets. I can't remember what any of us said. It began to get late and Charlie and Wanda suggested we should all stay in Bath for the night. I explained that I would get into trouble if I didn't get back that night. Brendan again said he would fix all that. The next morning Brendan was supposed to take me back to Oxford while Charlie and Wanda were to stay for an important meeting that Charlie had that night. Brendan said, 'But that's absurd, Charlie, there's a three-line Whip in the House tonight – you've got to get back for that'. So we all went back to Oxford, Brendan having furnished me with a doctor's certificate saying that it would be imprudent for me to have made a journey home through the night because of a sore throat.

This certificate was accepted with some dubiety by the senior Censor of Christ Church, Mr Gilbert Ryle. Charlie was not as fortunate as I was in taking Brendan's advice. When he got back to London he found that so far from there being a three-line whip Parliament was not even in session. He got into terrible trouble with his constituents, which culminated when Wanda in a hilarious moment threw a bun in a playful fashion at the Mayor of Bath. After this Charlie decided to abandon his political career. I think he was succeeded in the seat by Mr Loel Guinness.

In the summer of 1930 Brendan announced to his friends that he was inviting us all to stay at his Palazzo in Venice. None of us had ever heard that he had a Palazzo in Venice but he explained how he had recently inherited it from his mother. So the party consisted of Brendan, myself, Charlie and Wanda, and Gwen and Henry Mond, later Lord and Lady Melchett. Gwen and Henry had prudently decided to put up at the

Danielli Hotel. Brendan and I arrived first to open up the flat which was the top floor of a big modern palace just about opposite the Grand Hotel. I was rather surprised on arrival to see that the furniture was very Germanic and that all the books were in German. Brendan had excellent taste in eighteenth-century furniture. I asked him about this. He explained that late in life his mother had re-married a German and out of regard for her he did not care to change the décor.

I fear my first demand from my host was not to see the architectural splendours of Venice but to visit the Lido. Brendan agreed and insisted we go in a gondola. This took all of two hours. My impatience knew no bounds. Brendan said it would not take more than twenty minutes. We returned more expeditiously by motor-boat. Later the Baillie-Hamiltons and the Monds arrived, together with many other friends and we had a very merry three weeks; one of the gayest the English and American visitors had ever known in Venice; and there had been many before and, I suppose, since. It all ended up with a tremendous fracas on Murano, the Gondoliers Island. Insults were hurled, champagne bottles were brandished. Generally speaking everybody (without the excuse, for the most part, of being drunk) behaved with abandon.

It was a large dinner party to celebrate Lady Diana Cooper's birthday. Like most Venetian parties it did not start until about ten. Lady Cunard turned up about midnight and said, 'Has the party started?' I replied, 'It's ended, everyone is going home'. The news reverberated all over Venice and on the next day, it was said, a special train had to be chartered to convey back to England all the English nannies and governesses who had formerly been employed by the Italian aristocracy in the naïve belief that the English aristocracy was so much better brought up than their own.

Brendan was the best contact-man I have ever known. He knew an immense number of people in a wide circle of English and American life. He was thus able to discharge the most

RSC with Sir Harold Bowden riding pillion at the Motor Cycle
Show at Olympia: 30 November 1931

Lecture Tour of North
America: age 20,
winter 1931

Margaret Mercer-Nairne (now Lady
Margaret Myddelton)

RSC's 21st party. *R. to l.*: Lord Balniel (now Lord Crawford),
the late Lord Salisbury, WSC, Lord Birkenhead and Lord Hugh Cecil

RSC: age 21

useful function of passing on information between people operating usually at the highest levels of their professions. Though immensely talkative and apparently vastly indiscreet he seldom betrayed confidences that mattered. I remember one exquisite specimen of his technique.

It was the Sunday in September 1931 when, under the newly formed national government, Britain had to go off the gold standard. On the Saturday afternoon Brendan had seen Sir Ernest Harvey, deputy Governor of the Bank of England (the Governor, Mr Montagu Norman, was away in Canada: if he had been in London Brendan would certainly have seen him). He had spent the Saturday night at Merryworth in Kent as the guest of Mr Esmond Harmsworth (now Second Viscount Rothermere). He arrived at my father's house at Chartwell at about 11.30 on the Sunday with all the news of this shattering event which was exactly in opposition to the purposes for which the national government had been formed. We were all very struck by his lively account. My father invited him to stay to luncheon.

'No,' said Brendan, 'thank you very much but I must get on to Cherkley to tell Max about it and then on to see L.G. at Churt and discuss it with him. I will be back in London by eight and will call you then.'

Brendan at the time was the editor of the *Financial News*: so, of course, on the Monday morning he was in a position to call on the Chairman or Managing Directors of the big five banks in London: put them in the picture as to how all the politicians were reacting to these events: and be down in the smoking room of the House of Commons at 2.30 in the after-noon as the best-informed member of Parliament.

I never saw him do an equally magisterial job as he did that afternoon. But that was the pattern of life to which he aspired.

Basil Dufferin was the most lovable man I met at Oxford. His liquid spaniel eyes and his beautiful, charming manner, commanded affection. He was the most brilliant of all my contemporaries at Oxford. An undue addiction to drink blighted what might have been a fine political career. Later he took the cure but was never the same man afterwards. He perished tragically and unnecessarily in Burma in the last week of the war.

Basil had a caressing charm and it was always a delight to be in his company. One day he proposed to me that we should drive over to some village in the Cotswolds some twenty-five or thirty miles away where a great friend of his was completing his second novel. I don't think that I had heard at this time of the fabulous success that Evelyn Waugh had achieved with his first novel *Decline and Fall*, but Basil explained this to me while we were driving over. Evelyn must then have been engaged in writing his second novel *Vile Bodies*. We found him sitting outside a small country inn. He was dressed in a rough shirt and a pair of corduroy trousers and shod, I seem to remember, in sandals. It was a lovely day and we sat outside the pub drinking rum and water from large pewter tankards and eating bread and cheese.

This was my first encounter with this extraordinary and formidable little man. I cannot remember what we talked about or what impression he made on me but as soon as I got back to Oxford I obtained a copy of *Decline and Fall* and resolved to cultivate his acquaintance. This soon entered into a warm friendship which, though interrupted from time to time, has proved at the last enduring.

During my brief sojourn at Oxford, I managed to commit the most monumental social gaff of my career. A number of my friends and I had been invited to stay at Taplow by the hospitable Lady Desborough who always enjoyed mixing the generations. For some reason which I cannot recall, I came direct from London where I suppose I had had business of some sort or another and I was a good deal earlier than my companions from Oxford. A tea party of somewhat elderly ladies seemed to be in progress. I was invited to sit down. But, as is so often the English custom, no clear introductions were made. I found myself sitting next to what seemed to my youthful eyes to be a somewhat aged lady who asked me whether I knew Prof Lindemann. I said 'Yes, I do', and that he was a great friend of mine. She said 'Then why do so many people at Oxford say that the Prof is a snob?' I said, 'I think that's all a lot of rot; the other dons and professors are jealous of him because he has quite a lot of money and has a Mercedes-Benz. And of course,' I added, 'he does go to stay with frightfully dim people like the Portlands whom no one would visit unless they were Dukes.' My neighbour took this in very good part. A few moments later my friends arrived from Oxford. Too late for tea, they were gathered in the window drinking sherry. I excused myself from the tea table and joined my friends. After reciprocal salutations, I asked one of them who knew his way around, 'Who's that old trout over there?' He said, 'You bloody fool, it's the Duchess of Portland'. There was no way of explaining the matter or apologising for it. This was a Friday of a long weekend. Fortunately it was a large party and I never encountered the Duchess again. I have never been asked to Welbeck.

One of the enduring friendships I made in Oxford was with John Betjeman. I did not get to know him well at Oxford and our friendship was cemented later on. I remember how he took me one Sunday morning after church, which I had not attended, to have a sherry with a formidable character named Colonel Kolkhorst.

Suddenly in the middle of a company of forty or fifty people Betjeman stamped loudly on the floor and sang thuswise to the tune of John Peel:

> Do you ken Kolkhorst in his artful parlour
> Serving out the drink at his Sunday morning gala
> Some get sherry and some marsala
> With the arts and the crafts in the morning.

The refrain was taken up by all the company. I think it

must have been my first term at Oxford and I was naïvely astounded by the suave equanimity with which Colonel Kolkhorst received this eccentric outburst.

It was only later that I became an intimate and abiding friend of John Betjeman. For six months we shared a house in London which I rented for a peppercorn rent from Edward James. I was firm with Betjeman; I used to require him to write some verse every day when he returned from some degrading work he was doing in Fleet Street. Once he put down the following hilarious lines in about twenty minutes and recited them with his usual gusto:

> Ow what were you doing down 'arringay way
> I bought a bit of ribbon in the Bon Marche
> 'ome for supper or a 'ot 'igh tea
> Which Aunt Ena shall it be?
> Well soviets and serviettes are just the same to me
> So we'll split a pot per person in an ABC.

Edward James was a rich aesthete of most elegant appearance. I think he had left Oxford before I arrived but was a frequent visitor in his splendid Rolls-Royce. One day he brought down for a luncheon which I had organised Miss Tilly Losch whom he subsequently married. Miss Losch, who had been the prima ballerina in the Vienna State Opera, had recently come to London and had captured the town with her performances in *This Year of Grace* and later as the nun in *The Miracle*. She was at the height of her fame in England. Her beauty, her brilliant dancing and her delightful manners captivated everyone. I was enchanted by Tilly and her amusing Viennese accent. I remember the first conversational gambit I tried on her at my little luncheon party in my rooms at Canterbury (which I think had formerly been occupied by Edward James), began with a rather stilted question. I said, 'What was the first play you ever acted in?' She replied, 'It was a play by Villiam Shakespeare entitled "Finish good all good".' I guessed that she was translating literally from the German

All's well that ends well. A little later in the conversation, I asked her about her life in London and she said how she went to an underground station for the first time and 'rolled the stairs down'. She meant that she had come down on an escalator.

I took part in many debates in the Canning Club, of which I was a member and a regular attendant. Since my day it has been merged with the Chatham on which we always looked down. Now I am told that the joint club no longer possesses the fascination either of the Chatham or the Canning when they were independent institutions. These discussions were held in the rooms of the various undergraduate members, mulled claret was served, then someone read a paper and then there was discussion. Sometimes a Member of Parliament was invited down from London to address us. It was free and easy and companionable and a good informal background for the wider and more stylised audience of the Union.

Victor Cazalet turned out to be a most useful friend when he came down one day to address the Canning Club. I had already failed once in my history prelim and was coming up for examinations a second time. If I failed, I would be sent down, and this would have been excessively distasteful to my father. In my anxiety, I consulted Victor Cazalet and told him that the thing I was most worried about was the drawing of maps. It appeared that the examiners attached especial importance to this. He showed me in ten minutes how to draw a map of Italy; it was on the basis that if you put a dot at the top of the page for Milan, a dot halfway down for Rome and a dot at the bottom of the page for the eastern tip of Sicily, and drew a vertical line, it was easy to fill in the rough outline map of the Italian peninsula which it is often hard to remember does not run from North to South but from North-West to South-East. I found this extremely helpful and managed to introduce it into three separate papers which I understood were to be adjudicated by different examiners. I drew no other maps.

During one summer holidays I remember very well my father was most dissatisfied with my progress at my books at Oxford and insisted on employing a young don from Oxford to coach me for my forthcoming examinations. Prof Lindemann produced Mr Patrick Gordon-Walker who proved a most delightful companion and whose tuition did not prove unduly irksome in the summer holidays when one would much rather be doing other things than being locked up for two or three hours a day studying the *Gesta Francorum* or some other tedious work. However, he coached well and I successfully passed my examination later in the year. I think Gordon-Walker must have picked up a thing or two from my father over luncheon and dinner; because he briefly became Foreign Secretary in the new Labour Government.

My history tutor at the House had grown dissatisfied with my laziness and indifferent essays I read to him each week. He said shortly before the examinations, 'I've a very good mind to write to the examiners and tell them that you are unfit to sit for the examination'. I was not prepared to put up with this sort of rot and formally withdrew myself from his tuition.

I sought out my friend Lord David Cecil. He was good enough to come and have lunch with me in my rooms at Canterbury for the three successive days before the examination. Unlike my history tutor, he did not try to expose my ignorance. He produced several specimen examination papers with ten or twelve questions on them of which one only had to answer four or five, and asked me which ones I knew most about, or on which I was not entirely uninformed. He proceeded to fill in the gaps, draw to my attention useful dates and useful quotations. With his help and that of Victor Cazalet's map of Italy, I cantered easily through this ordeal, to the vast mortification of my history tutor who had gone on strike.

I paid little attention to my books at Oxford. I don't think I ever attended a lecture. I longed to shine in the Oxford Union and made a number of speeches there. Eventually I was accorded the privilege of being 'put on the paper', ie of delivering one of the four major speeches with which the debate begins, when there is always a good audience. The debate was to be about the new minority Socialist Government's plans for Egypt which had been preceded by the dismissal from Egypt of my father's old friend Sir George Lloyd. I was, I think, seconding the vote of censure on His Majesty's Government. I had taken a lot of pains about my speech and was dismayed to hear a few days before the debate was to be held that Quintin Hogg, a former President of the Union, intended to move the adjournment of the Union just so that this debate would fall to the ground. Those of my way of thinking thought that Quintin was being tiresome and self-important. His view was that it was not in the national interest that the Oxford Union should pronounce an adverse view or indeed any view at all upon this grave Imperial question.

I consulted Freddie and he said, 'Why don't you go up to London and consult my father?' This I did. Lord Birkenhead received me with great ceremony in his handsome room in Thames House which he occupied in his capacity as Chairman of the Greater London Electrical Counties Trust. I told him of my predicament and he said 'Would you like me to suggest a method by which you should oppose Quintin?' I said, 'Yes please'. He rang for a secretary and in a few moments dictated me some notes. The line of argument he suggested was that it was unlikely that our youthful lucubrations would have any serious reverberations through the teeming bazaars of the East, etc., etc. I hastened back to Oxford, put on my tail-coat and white tie which in those days were obligatory when speaking on the paper. My friends and I succeeded in defeating Quintin who retired with his friends in their dudgeons from the hall.

Though the debate failed to produce any repercussions or reverberations in the 'teeming bazaars of the East', it made some impact in the United States and markedly changed my way of life. This debate was held at the height of the 'silly season' and so a number of London newspapers sent down special correspondents to report it. The *News Chronicle* in particular wrote a favourable account of my oratorical prowess and reported the debate in splash banner headline on the front page entitled 'Reporting a Parliament of Youth'. This report was picked up by the *New York Times*, who made something of it.

A week or ten days later, I was lying in bed about 10.30 in the morning when my great American friend Boy Sheftel passed by my rooms in Canterbury Quad suitably gowned on his way to a lecture. He said, 'You haven't opened your mail'. 'No,' I said. He said, 'There's one here from America, shall I open it for you?' I said, 'Please do'. He opened it and exclaimed, 'Good God. It's an invitation to make a lecture tour in the United States'.

I was still feeling somewhat lethargic from the evening's exertions and did not betray much interest save to say, 'Do they offer to pay?' 'Yes,' he said, 'Quite a lot of money.' I sat up and read this letter from a respected firm of lecture agents – William B. Feakins, Inc.

At the time I subsisted on an allowance, given me by my father, of four hundred pounds a year. This was about the average that undergraduates had at that time. This probably did not apply to the whole University but to undergraduates at the House who were, on the whole, better off than most. I was in debt to the extent of six hundred or seven hundred pounds and was by no means living within my means. The idea of going off to America and teaching, rather than learning appealed to me strongly, and I resolved to go. Everybody except my father thought I was crazy; he encouraged me to embark on the venture. So in a few weeks I sailed to the United States on the *SS Berengaria* – or perhaps it was the *Majestic*.

Some weeks before I left my father enquired whether I had yet composed my lectures. I said no, I would do that during the

three weeks which I was planning to spend in Venice. He
chuckled. When I came back from Venice, on the eve of my
departure for the United States, my father enquired what
progress I had made. I said, 'I'm afraid not much, I'm going to
do it on the ship'. 'Ah,' he said, 'the first day you are on the
ship you won't be feeling very well, the second day you will
be feeling better, the third day you will meet a pretty girl and
then you will be nearly there.'

Thus it turned out, but I consoled myself by thinking there
was a whole week after I got to America before I would have
to deliver my first lecture. However, when we docked, I was
met by my lecture agent, Mr Feakins, who said he had just
managed to fit in an extra lecture which I was to deliver that
evening at Princeton University. So the time was up. Mr
Feakins stressed the importance of this lecture. He said a lot of
the press would be there and the reports they made on it would
affect the whole outcome of my three-month tour. I tried to
look unconcerned but I'm bound to say I felt distinctly queasy.

The late Mr William Randolph Hearst, with whom my
father and I had stayed the previous summer at San Simeon,
had very kindly sent his top gossip columnist Mr Maury Paul,
who wrote under the name of Cholly Knickerbocker, to meet
me; he suggested driving me down to Princeton and so the
opportunity which I had hoped to have had to prepare something in the train was denied to me. We chatted merrily all the
way.

My recollection of the lecture is somewhat of a blur. I had
three alternative subjects:

1 Why I am not a Socialist?
2 Can Youth be Conservative?
3 The British Empire and World Progress.

It seemed to me the same lecture; adaptations could be
made on any of these three subjects but I did not even have the
material for one.

When I was led on to the platform and introduced by the chairman it appeared there was a very distinguished audience in the body of the Kirk, notably Monsieur André Maurois who was doing a temporary stint as a professor at the university. I cannot remember which topic had been selected by the authorities at Princeton. That didn't matter – I said everything I could that appeared relevant to the issue, whatever that may have been, looked at my watch and found that I had only been going twenty minutes. I was supposed to speak for a full hour; so I took a deep breath and produced a lot of stuff wholly irrelevant to the subject that I was supposed to be speaking on and looked at my watch and found that I had still only been speaking for thirty minutes. I took another big breath and did what in retrospect must have been a brilliant recapitulation, in other words, of what I had already said, no doubt introducing the phrase 'To sum up then'. I looked at my watch and it said forty minutes. I had no more to say. I sat down convinced that my lecture tour would have to be abandoned amidst the derision of the press.

A little later I discovered that my watch had stopped in the middle of the lecture and that I had regaled my audience for no less than one hour and a quarter with my unconsidered improvised oratory. Perhaps they had nothing better to do.

The newspaper reports were flattering – even gushing – and I strode on through the Middle West from triumph to triumph.

I had obtained a term's leave of absence from the House, that most indulgent and comprehending of all academic institutions; but the lecture tour was such a success that though it was only planned for three months, the admirable Mr Feakins proposed a second three months which involved two terms of absence. The House, however, did not seem to complain about this. I was still only nineteen but I enjoyed my new-found freedom and what seemed great affluence so much that I could not bear the idea of going back to Oxford again on the allowance which was all that my father could afford. I of course spent all, perhaps rather more than all of the twelve thousand dollars which I had earned in the lecture tour during the seven months that I was there. I had very grand ideas in those days and I invariably reserved a suite at the hotels I visited. When there was a gap of three or four days between lectures I did not hesitate to fly back to New York or more often to Cleveland where I had formed an attachment which has been lifelong with a charming girl who resided at that time in that city. And when I came to leave the United States I was still owing about two thousand dollars.

This confirmed me in the view that it would be imprudent to return to the delights of Oxford. I had been there for four terms and had profited from it in many ways. I had learnt a lot about life and I had made many friends, but I felt that I was a grown-up man and they were still silly boys, and that I was prepared to embark on the battle of life.

When I went to Oxford some of my older friends like Duff Cooper said, 'Of course Oxford's not what it was before the First War and you won't find that it has any of the glamour and enchantment that it then possessed'. I told the same story to my son Winston when he went up to the House after the Second World War. Well of course, things aren't what they used to be but most of the essential things go on. It is a wonderful atmosphere and arena in which to test one's wits against cleverer people than oneself. You find out how much you can drink without disgracing yourself and learn how to associate in a civilised way with people of all ages and all classes. It provides also a marvellous arena in which to learn to think and speak coherently on your feet, a task in my view which should be mastered by any man whether he aspires to enter public life or not.

My father did not like the idea of my leaving Oxford and said that as I was ill-equipped for any profession I must get a job before he could consent to this proposal. I consulted my great new friend Henry Mond, who was shortly to succeed his father as second Lord Melchett. He was a director of ICI and he suggested that I should go and be assistant editor on the ICI house magazine. I informed my father of this and he said that he would like to have a talk with Henry, whom he knew well, as to the prospects. My father and I met Henry somewhere in the country. Henry was accompanied by his wife Gwen, who like Henry was also a great friend of mine. Henry, my father and I took a walk in the garden where Henry eloquently explained the glittering prospects that lay ahead for a young man of twenty who joined this great company. But what really impressed my father was looking in the dining window as we walked into the garden and seeing Gwen sitting there absolutely immobile and statuesque. He agreed to what Henry proposed and driving back he did not discuss the matter with me. Instead he expatiated on how impressed he had been by Gwen. 'It is a very rare thing,' he said, 'to see a woman capable of such majestic tranquillity and silence.' I was fully of the same opinion.

I did not enjoy working at ICI. I was not good at the job; I did not like office hours and indeed was bad at keeping them. It was a justification for leaving Oxford and brought me in a small income which I supplemented by occasional articles in the Sunday newspapers. I also undertook a lecture tour on my experiences in the United States. This brought in quite a bit of money. Thus I subsisted for about a year, getting acquainted with London and with its social scene.

On 28 May 1932 I celebrated my twenty-first birthday. My father hit on the happy and original idea of giving a dinner party for me a few days later at Claridges, and the idea was 'Fathers and Sons'. It was a splendid occasion and far more than I deserved. The occasion was more suited to my pretensions than to my achievements or abilities.

I think it is best described in two extracts from contemporary newspapers. The next morning the *Evening Standard* printed the following anonymous paragraphs in the 'Londoner's Diary'.

Evening Standard
17 June 1932

'GREAT' MEN AND THEIR SONS

Mr Churchill gave a dinner to his son last night. The company consisted of many men who are called great and also their sons. These 'great' men are convinced, needless to say, that their sons are also 'great'. The sons, or most of them, admire their parents' judgment in this respect. Missing from the list was Mr Baldwin and Mr Baldwin's son Oliver.

Everybody was filled with curiosity about the 'boys'. Yet Mr Churchill put up some of the old codgers to make speeches, and he made a very good one himself.

It was not short, but it was substantial. He spoke of the torch, the flag and the lamp. If anyone else had taken that subject you could fill in the spaces for yourself. But, of course, you could not do that with Mr Churchill. He adorned the theme, as usual.

But what of the younger generation? Lord Birkenhead (aged twenty-four) made a grand speech, carefully prepared, word perfect, witty, with phraseology reminiscent of his father. It was a considerable improvement on the last time I heard him at his own twenty-first birthday, though he was brilliant on that occasion, too.

If oratory is to determine political position in the future, as in the past, then Lord Birkenhead's success is assured.

Randolph Churchill (aged twenty-one) was best described by his own father, who, in speaking of his fluency, said he was a fine machine-gun, and it was to be hoped he would accumulate a big dump of ammunition and learn to hit the target.

Not a word of Randolph Churchill's speech was prepared, but there was ample evidence of fine natural abilities. To him an old codger may say 'Work, my boy, work! The way is wide open to you in politics if you do!'

The Hon Quintin Hogg (aged twenty-four): a very fine speech, with not too much evidence of preparation; an easy passing from gay to grave; finished in form; a shade too nervous in delivery. If his judgment on other issues is as sound as it is on material for speeches, he will go to the top in the House of Commons provided Lord Hailsham lives long enough.

The last of the quartet who were allowed to provide interludes in the oratory of their elders was to me one of the most interesting. He was the Hon Seymour Berry (aged twenty-two).

His speaking had neither the finished form of the others nor their conscious assurance in addressing an audience. Yet it would not surprise me if he went as far as any of them.

For he possesses that quality which is above all others valuable in a public man – the impression of absolute sincerity.

I was only twenty-one but I knew enough of the world and of Fleet Street and of Beaverbrook to detect the hand of the Lord. The other notice of the occasion which is worth recalling was printed five days later in the *Sunday Times* signed at the foot D. and A. This was my friend Basil Dufferin. It was the view of a younger man than Lord Beaverbrook and possibly more sympathetic, though none the less penetrating. This is what he wrote:

Sunday Times
19 June 1932

To have, perforce, a distinguished father is no light handicap for a young man intent on making his own way in the world. His failures are accentuated by comparison; his successes explained away by heredity.

Nevertheless, on Thursday evening there was an opportunity of observing how the younger generation is coping with the difficulty. The occasion was a dinner party given by Mr Winston Churchill to celebrate the coming-of-age of his son Randolph.

The original purpose of the host was that each distinguished guest should establish his credentials by bringing with him his son, but fortunately the rigour of this rule was considerably relaxed, or else many of those present would have missed a memorable evening.

Nevertheless the original idea was often adhered to: Lord Hailsham, for instance, came with Mr Quintin Hogg, Lord Reading with Lord Erleigh, Lord Rothermere with Mr Esmond Harmsworth, and so through a long list of famous men; and each man there no doubt hopes that he will live to receive an invitation to a similar function on the name and fame of his son.

The reputation of Mr Churchill stands second to none for gifts of hospitality and friendship, and it is doubtful if any other man in England could have entertained a gathering more representative of every sphere of the mind's activity. Nor, fortunately, was the light of these planets dimmed by any of those flashing meteors of sport, films, or aviation, who looking alike but answering to different names, impose such a strain upon the memory of individuals.

But the occasion was in reality more noteworthy than the celebration of a birthday, graced by however distinguished a company. Rather, it afforded a common meeting ground on which those separated by years, outlook, and upbringing might discuss the differences between them, and assure each other of the underlying sympathy with which the one regards even the most doubtful activities of the other.

It was an opportunity for young men; and of young men we will speak.

Lord Birkenhead rose to propose the health of Mr Randolph Churchill. As his father before him he prefers the snowy spectacle of the tablecloth to the nauseous appearance of his audience. With head down, in a clear musical monotone, he made a speech that would not have impaired the reputation of any present.

The savage irony, the adroit turn of phrase, the suave compliment that turned like a flash into a deadly weapon of assault, reminded one irresistibly of his father. It was not the usual speech on such occasions; his respect for Mr Randolph Churchill had to be inferred rather than applauded. Lord Birkenhead lacks as yet the urbanity that softened his father's jests; but it was a speech that few young men would have dared to risk in such company, and the risk came off.

Only by the moderation of his language did Mr Randolph Churchill betray his sense of the importance of the occasion. Speaking, as is his custom, impromptu, with great wealth of gesture and fluency of delivery, one could not doubt his ability, even if one questioned his sentiments. With all the energy and brains of the Churchills, lacking only as yet coherence of ideas, he has almost all the qualities that make for success.

It was curious to hear a young man, only just of age, yet whose writings and lectures were discussed, if not approved, throughout a continent and whose earnings are a matter for envious speculation, ask humbly and correctly for the leadership and advice of the older generation. He is probably right, but it is a new and recently acquired wisdom.

Three other young speakers must be mentioned.

Quintin Hogg, another practised orator, with jaw outthrust, and flashing eyes, intensely emotional, fiercely combative, is a personality one cannot forget. One imagines that his father once used the same methods: and is it Time or the security of the Front Bench that can change the roarings of this lion into the mellifluous cooing of the dove?

Then, a very different type, Mr Seymour Berry. Here there is none of that anxiety for success that marks the young politician or lawyer.

Despising the usual aids of oratory – gesture, inflection, rhetoric, one felt perhaps that of all these young men he was most sure of the ground on which he stood. Perhaps it is because the aims and alliances of the young man in business are simple and easy to determine, whereas the aims and alliances of the young politician are vague and continually changing, that he alone could remain calm and almost aloof.

The last of these young men was Mr Esmond Harmsworth, older than the others, and smilingly confessing that he was not sure to which generation he does belong. He is a practised speaker, and in happy phrase, with the ring of sincerity, he expressed the best wishes for Randolph's future.

To the onslaught of this powerful team the older generation replied confidently enough. Sir Austen Chamberlain, before whom criticism wilts; Lord Hugh Cecil, performing that rare feat in oratory of finishing his sentences; the Duke of Marlborough, happy of phrase; Lord Hailsham, one of our very best speakers; Mr Churchill himself, younger and more vigorous of speech than any of his guests – all these contributed nobly to make the evening almost historic. It is not often that one has the chance of comparing the methods of five of the best orators in England in one evening.

And so, as the room filled with cigar smoke, and the decanter pursued its amiable path, one was compelled to contemplate, without originality, but with great comfort to oneself, how remarkable a thing it is that breeding in horses and dogs is so respected, and in men it is so disregarded.

Of all those who spoke that evening there was not one who could not trace his gifts directly to an ancestral source. It seems that many of those sources are still capable of producing men as competent as their fathers in the management of their lives, and possibly of the lives of others.

D. and A.

A few weeks after this splendid dinner in my honour I flew to Berlin to cover the German elections for the *Sunday Graphic* – a paper now defunct. Looking at my files I see that I reported on 31 July 1932:

... Nothing is more foolish than to underestimate the intensely vital spirit that animates the Nazi movement. Hitler has no detailed policy. He has promised all things to all men. Many Germans say that he no longer wants power – that he is frightened of the forces he has called into being. They say he does not want a majority and merely wishes to be part of a Coalition. I do not believe this to be true.

He is surrounded by a group of resolute, tough and vehement men who would never tolerate any backsliding from their leader. Nothing can long delay their arrival in power. Hitler will not betray them. But let us make no mistake about it.

The success of the Nazi party sooner or later means war. Nearly all of Hitler's principal lieutenants fought in the last war. Most of them have two or three medals on their breasts. They burn for revenge. They are determined once more to have an army. I am sure that once they have achieved it they will not hesitate to use it.

For the moment, however, the danger is postponed. It is virtually impossible for Hitler to win this election. He will have to continue his support of the present Government.

In the last twelve months there have been four elections, which have cost Germany over £6,000,000. They cannot afford another one yet, but all the time the Nazis will attain strength and impetus, and within three years at the most Europe will be confronted with a deadly situation.

It would be vain to pretend that I thought all this out for myself; but I had sat for many years at the feet of my father. When I went to Berlin two months after my twenty-first birthday I found ample proof of his fears. I was to spend the next thirteen years of my life in the Hitler era. I am proud that I got off to a good start.

EPILOGUE 1964

WHEN some parts of this book were serialised at the end of the year, the *Sunday Times* used as a curtain-raiser a recorded interview between Mr Clive Irving, their Managing Editor, and myself. The object of the interview was to bring out how I feel today more than thirty years after the close of the book. What mistakes I made, how my thoughts and ideas have since matured and generally speaking what sort of a person I am today in my fifty-fourth year. For the purpose of this book it was thought more appropriate to use the material that follows as an epilogue rather than a prologue.

IRVING: How high were your ambitions at the age of twenty-one?

CHURCHILL: Oh, very high indeed. I always assumed from the time I was thirteen or fourteen that the only career for me was politics, like my father and grandfather – if anyone had said to me that I wouldn't get to be in the House of Commons by the time I was twenty-one, or immediately afterwards, I would have thought them absolutely too ridiculous for words. This nascent and unwarranted ambition was partly prompted by the fact that I had the same birthday, May 28, as the younger Pitt, and I was very apt to keep writing down the fact that he had the same birthday as mine. If he could be Chancellor of the Exchequer at twenty-three and Prime Minister at twenty-five I saw no reason why I shouldn't do the same. But, of course, later events showed that this was not in one's power to command, and I had to wait. Of course, now, these many years, I've been deprived of all political ambitions and I'm deeply absorbed in writing the life of my father, and I've taken to gardening in middle age. When you get the gardening bug in middle age you get it very badly. And I've formed a deep aversion to London. And, of course, if one was in the House of Commons one would have to go to that dreadful place. Quite often, I suppose. And then one would have to go to one's constituency, too – even more odious, although that would depend on the constituency. But, anyway, there's no rush of people asking me to go into Parliament, and it really suits me very well. I've found it's not a question of sour grapes. I mean, up to the time I was forty years old I ardently aspired to be a member of Parliament but I only achieved it for five years in the war and I was overseas most of the time. I only made three or four speeches and, anyway, I frankly don't think the House of Commons is what it used to be. I think I would have had a lot of fun there if I had got there in time. But I decided to turn my back on that.

IRVING: You may not be a politician now, but you manage to lead an intensely political life, don't you?

CHURCHILL: Well, of course. I was brought up to it and took it in with my mother's milk. I was practically born on a political platform. And, of course, I follow it all very closely and I like to express my views on it from time to time, but it's just as useful doing it in public print or occasionally on television as it would be waiting three days to make a speech in the House of Commons and not being called, which must be one of the most frustrating experiences in the world.

IRVING: Do you think strong personalities like yourself find it possible to get on in politics today?

CHURCHILL: Well, I don't think so. Both parties seem to resent the idea of anyone carving out a political career of their own. The idea – Baldwin really started it all – is that you rise by steady, obedient service to the party. The idea

118

that you should strike out on your own, express your own views and try perhaps to convert your own party to those views, as Lord Randolph did, as my father did (the latter with possibly more success than my grandfather had) – all this seems deeply revolting to the modern age. People say it's all the fault of the Whips. I think that's a cowardly and defeatest explanation. No one need be frightened of the Whips. The trouble is they all want to get on and the Whips always make it difficult for people to get on except through assiduous sucking up.

But there have been people who've broken away from that. If you can make yourself necessary to a party . . . well, they can't do without you, they can't dispense with you. The first Lord Melchett, Sir Alfred Mond, took as the motto on his crest when he was ennobled the very sensible words 'Make yourself necessary'. Anyone who makes himself necessary and if possible indispensable soon commands his own terms in politics as much as in any other field.

IRVING: Do you think that women have been bad for politics? They've made language much too polite?

CHURCHILL: Yes, certainly. I think the whole art of political invective is dead, the days of great oratory are over, women are so easily shocked. 'I don't think that's very *nice*', they say. But obviously the women's vote is here to stay. It's always struck me as a great mistake on their part. The influence of women is only successful when it's indirect.

IRVING: Then it can be quite influential.

CHURCHILL: Oh, certainly, so long as it's exercised in country houses, at the dining-room table, in the boudoir and the bedroom, it can often be very beneficial. But I believe with Dr Johnson. 'A woman talking is like a dog walking on its hind legs. It is not done well, sir, but one marvels that it's done at all.' Curiously enough, the better a woman speaks the more embarrassing I always find it. It makes me feel quite uncomfortable.

IRVING: That must be one of the few things that manage to make you feel uncomfortable.

CHURCHILL: I think a woman must learn to be a good listener.

IRVING: Who would you say has been the most influential woman politically in this country in the last fifty years?

CHURCHILL: Margot Asquith, who worked behind the scenes, certainly had much more influence than Nancy Astor did. There's a moral in that for all women, although they were somewhat similar in their outspokenness. But Margot did it behind the scenes.

IRVING: Do you think the two-party system has become a bad thing?

CHURCHILL: Well, I don't quite think that. People say we've always had a three-party system. It really isn't true. The Irish thing, of course, bedevilled our politics for a hundred years. But since the rise of the Labour Party and the gradual withering away of the Liberal Party, it is now a two-party system. I don't see why that should necessarily lead to an increase in the greater approximation between the views of the two parties. I think it's because there are no great and tremendous issues any longer. The lack of great issues means the lack of great personalities to champion them, and we are, after all, I think, a very great country with the best system of government in the world.

I was born a Liberal but the Liberal Party came to an end. My father and I both decided our duty was to join the Conservative Party in order to maintain Britain's liberal heritage against the onrushing tides of totalitarian Socialism. One of the reasons the Liberal Party came to an end, apart from the terrible bitterness which arose between the Asquith and Lloyd George families, was really that it had achieved all it set out to do, and now there isn't a very great deal more to be done. Of course, things can be improved. But basically what's important is to preserve our liberal heritage. That is the foundation of my political thinking.

120

Stour, East Bergholt

RSC today

IRVING: It seems to me that the Conservative Party today often finds your views as difficult to accommodate as the Labour Party does. You don't fulfil anyone's idea of a stereotyped Conservative – you wouldn't see yourself as that, would you?

CHURCHILL: No – well, I don't really consider myself a member of the Tory Party. I'm a buttress rather than a pillar. I don't admire everything about the Conservative Party. I don't admire all their leaders. But I do think they're a very much better lot than the other side. But on the whole – it's easier doing this living in the country – I prefer the detached and I think quite objective view about politics. I'm really an onlooker and a commentator: I'm not a violent partisan.

IRVING: Your family can't be regarded as part of the Tory establishment in any way, can it?

CHURCHILL: I suppose we're partly of the establishment and partly anti-establishment. I suppose from Lord Randolph downwards we've usually had a foot in both camps.

IRVING: But you did see this establishment very much at work last October, didn't you? The idea that the decision in the end is always going to be taken by the people who choose the man because he suits them rather than the needs of the day.

CHURCHILL: But the needs of the day broadly corresponded to the needs of the Tory Party. I don't like the use of the word 'establishment' in this connection because what is intended by the establishment is the Archbishop of Canterbury, *The Times* newspaper, the BBC and all that crowd. They have nothing whatsoever to do with the selection of the leader of the Tory Party. What was proven in the week after Blackpool is that the decision was made by the country gentlemen of England. I suppose it's probably a bad thing to say just now. But they were the last resort: I don't know how long it will continue, and they have the power of selecting a leader. They certainly had the power at Blackpool to get rid of one they didn't like. This red-brick university legend that Macleod and Maudling tried to build up and thrive on was proven to be a hollow sham, because of course the true hierarchy of the Tory Party – it isn't a hierarchy really, it's very varied ... but one of the reasons they survived in our party institution is that they've always welcomed into their arms men of talent, wherever they've come from. Look at Disraeli: the gentlemen of England embraced him – ardently, as a man might embrace his mistress – because they saw he could do their work better for them than they could do it themselves. They are a pragmatic party and they choose whatever seems most expedient in the interests of the country and no doubt in their own interests at the time. Well, they don't always choose right but there is no doubt they have a considerable power of decision.

IRVING: You started out with these enormous political ambitions. Why do you think that they never came to anything?

CHURCHILL: Well, I suppose a country usually finds it's an inconvenience except in a major war having a Churchill around and to have two barging around at the same time I suppose is felt to be doubly inconvenient. I loyally embraced, with conviction, all my father's causes, but I then blotted my copybook with the Conservative Central Office by going and fighting a by-election in 1935 at Wavertree and neatly splitting the Tory vote in half and letting the Socialist in. And I don't think I've ever really been forgiven for that. I don't think the Central Office may remember what it was about but there is a sort of vague black mark in their minds. For many years it went on, but now that I've abandoned all political ambitions I find them very helpful and co-operative people.

But I think my father was big enough and sufficiently well known with his immense genius and power of self-expression – he was able to weather the storm and survive in those difficult and unhappy years in the 'thirties, when he was immensely isolated. But in the nature of things there wasn't room for me. I'm not making excuses – it was largely my own fault, but I think it was a handicap to me and, of course, I'm not very good at kissing babies and I don't tolerate fools very gladly, and I didn't really get on terribly well with most of the devoted party workers in the various constituencies which I invited to return me to Parliament.

IRVING: Did you find it very difficult to assert some kind of separate personality from your father's, although you in fact believed in the same ideals?

CHURCHILL: Well, yes, I suppose that was partly my trouble really. Much as I revered and reverenced him I wasn't prepared just to be an ADC and go along, I wanted to have a show of my own. So, struggling to establish my own individuality and personality I often said and wrote rather reckless things, which I suppose if I hadn't felt this frustration I would have tempered down. I suppose I am a markedly extrovert person and I like to cultivate and display my own personality. I try and think things out for myself. Substantially I went along with my father all the way, but I was always looking for opportunities to establish an individual position, and it's very hard to do so, obviously, when you're living under the shadow of the great oak tree – the small sapling, so close to the parent tree, doesn't perhaps receive enough sunshine. Of course, I had wonderful opportunities and to begin with everyone was very kind and helpful to me. But I became sort of bloody-minded, I suppose, and wanted to strike out on my own and adopted possibly rather an arrogant attitude towards people and institutions at a time when I didn't really have the ammunition or the skill to hit the target. But I hold neither guilt feelings nor reproaches about that. I think anyone can see that there were difficulties naturally inherent in the situation.

IRVING: Who were your friends in that period?

CHURCHILL: I shall actually be writing about that in my autobiography, which you're going to serialise very shortly. My main friends, I suppose, were Seymour Berry, my cousin Tom Mitford, Freddie Birkenhead, Brendan Bracken, Charlie Baillie-Hamilton – who died too young and had immense charm. I moved in rather a small circle really because when we had the India row and the Defence row and Munich and all that I insulted everybody who was taking what I conceived to be a defeatist view. I daresay this was rather embarrassing to my father because though he fought these issues very stoutly he was always very careful to maintain urbane relations with people of all views. But I rather charged out in every way, and was apt to attack people on any favourable occasion – a private dinner-party, a country house-party or in a club – and so I rapidly lost friends and such abilities as I had to influence people. After the war, I had to start again, but of course I learnt a lot from it. I trust I'm still reasonably aggressive, but I begin to think I'm getting my head above water again.

IRVING: You've given up London life more or less completely, haven't you?

CHURCHILL: Yes, really completely. I only go there when I have to go there. And I can usually get back in a day, thanks to that admirable man, Dr Beeching, who has so much improved our local train services. If I have to spend the night in town I hurry back as soon as possible. I doubt if on the average over the last three years I've spent more than one night a month in London.

IRVING: You were so much part of London life. Don't you miss it?

CHURCHILL: No, not a bit. You can't lead the sort of London life I used to lead. You can't get around the place.

IRVING: Do you think it's you that's changed or London?

CHURCHILL: Well, both. I suppose I've changed more than London has. Immediately after the Coronation I committed myself to writing the life of the late Lord Derby and I realised

124

I couldn't possibly do it in London and so I took a house in the country, a lovely house called Oving, looking over the vale of Aylesbury. It's now the home of Mr Michael and Lady Pamela Berry. I was there for a year and when I went there all my friends said, 'Oh, what rot, Randolph going to live in the country. He'll be up two or three times a week. We'll see him hanging round the bar at White's'. But I found that I liked the country life and I found I could get on with my work much better and London became less and less attractive to me. So I then persuaded my trustees to buy me a house in the country. I spent six or seven months looking for a suitable place and then stumbled on Stour. Here I've been now about eight years and I've put my roots down.

IRVING: How did you stumble on it?

CHURCHILL: Well, because I suppose I'd looked at forty or fifty houses. I was married then and we thought we'd like to live in Kent or Sussex or Wiltshire, but all those houses we looked at were either too big or too expensive or too small. I hadn't looked in East Anglia at all, I had rather a thing against East Anglia. I used to stay a lot in my early youth with my cousin Venetia Montagu at Beccles which is a very bleak part of Suffolk, blasted moors, pine trees, not at all an English setting and rather flat, and though I delighted in going there because many of my greatest friends were usually there I formed a prejudice against it, I suppose. So East Anglia was the last place we looked at. By this time we got pretty narky about the advertisements and particulars you get from the house agents and we didn't waste much time going to unsuitable houses. When we saw that it said 'somewhat overlarge kitchen wing could of course be pulled down without expense,' well, we smelt a rat and we didn't bother to go there.

We came down here one day and within five minutes of coming into the house decided this was it. It was the right size, it had this beautiful view, not so extensive as Oving had;

it is a smaller and more domesticated view, across the Stour river with the famous square tower of Dedham Church which Constable was always painting the most prominent feature of the landscape. And here I am. And here I mean to stay.

IRVING: You are certainly a dedicated countryman and yet you still manage to maintain constant contact with everything that's going on in London that you need to know about?

CHURCHILL: Well, many of my friends are good enough to come down here. And of course I make very extensive use of the telephone.

IRVING: What's your quarterly telephone bill now?

CHURCHILL: About £300 I should think.

IRVING: How often do you call the United States?

CHURCHILL: I don't know, it depends. If there's something exciting going on and I want to know about it I may make four or five calls in a day. Very often I don't call for a month. It's pure caprice.

IRVING: You manage to get the best of both worlds, you have this elaborate intelligence service and at the same time you have the peace of the country to concentrate in.

CHURCHILL: I remember the late Lord Beaverbrook once saying to me: 'Well, of course at heart I'm just an old concierge. I like to know what's going on.' Well, I think I'm a sort of middle-aged concierge. I have a great desire to know what's going on.

IRVING: Do you relish the thought of all these manager figures appearing in politics?

CHURCHILL: Well, someone's got to manage it. But I'd like to see things managed by statesmen long-tried in the public service. I don't think the country ought to be governed by people no one really knows anything about, except that some group of people say they've got a first-class brain and that sort of thing. I think politics should be run by the people

126

who've carved out an individual and independent position for themselves in the life of the nation. And not these faceless men who have no real accountability, whom no one knows anything about. I can't bear the idea of falling into the hands of experts or scientists or people like that.

IRVING: But you're very pleased with what Dr Beeching has done with the railways.

CHURCHILL: I am indeed. But we're talking about politics. Of course, you've got to have managers in business, even in nationalised undertakings you must have the best business management you can find. But I don't think they should sit in the Cabinet. Experts must always be firmly controlled by men with rather perhaps less nimble and exact minds but men with broader minds and well-established characters.

IRVING: Your father had a lot of people round him in the war who today would be called managers, who were at the time some of them unorthodox.

CHURCHILL: Well, once he said 'scientists should be on tap, but not on top' – a little-known remark of his.

IRVING: You think he had his scientists under control? What about Lindemann – don't you think he got a bit too much influence?

CHURCHILL: He was never allowed to interfere in politics; I often heard my father say to him. 'Now, now, Prof, that's politics. You mustn't interfere in that.' He did have a lot of influence because he was able to translate complicated scientific facts and theories in a way my father could understand. My father was not of a scientific bent of mind, any more than I am. But it was very convenient when you have to take decisions on these things to have someone who can explain them to you. He happened to be a very long-standing friend of my father and he'd worked with him in all the rearmament campaigns between the two wars and was already ready with his slide rule to work out what the Germans were up to and that sort of thing. He was a most invaluable part of my father's small team who tried to get our country ready for the war.

IRVING: You're in rather a unique position in that you've worked for practically every newspaper. Is there any newspaper group that you haven't worked for?

CHURCHILL: I haven't worked for the *Daily Worker*. But I don't admit that I work for papers. They work for me. I write articles, they pay me well for them and they go to the enormous labour and expense of setting them up in type, of printing them and distributing them all over the country. I'm not really doing the work, they're doing the work. I find it a pleasure to write and I'm very glad there are still one or two people who are prepared to print what I have to say. But I think that's a very slavish attitude for a journalist to adopt. What's this phrase they always say in Fleet Street about the 'working' Press? Apparently, by the working Press they don't mean anyone who works with his brain and tries to concentrate on good writing. It means men who stand in dirty mackintoshes outside people's houses where they're not wanted and try to accost them as they come in and out. If that's what working for a paper means you can include me out.

IRVING: Among all the newspapers that you've written for at one time or another you've known all the Press proprietors, and I think from time to time you have attacked them all. Do you think there is any hope of reformation?

CHURCHILL: Well, I live in hopes. I go battling on. But it's very hard work and one gets very little support. The thing I resent so much is that they stand such a way above the law. They can criticise anybody but they get awfully sensitive and upset if anyone criticises them. And of course they hardly ever criticise each other. It's all part of their cartel arrangement they call dog don't eat dog. I prefer to call it son of a bitch don't eat son of a bitch. I think that sort of power does corrupt people. They're so sensitive about any intrusion on their private lives yet they seem utterly insensitive about hiring people to go and do it to all their readers and fellow countrymen. I think it's a very unlovely and degrading spectacle, and I think some progress is being made toward stopping that.

IRVING: Do you think the standard of writing in newspapers in this country is still higher than it is in the United States?

CHURCHILL: Yes, I think it is. I don't like the American idiom, the way they take up these vogue words. Five years ago you couldn't read an American columnist that didn't have the word 'viable' in it. Now they've gone and corrupted the word 'compounded' to make it mean almost exactly the opposite to what it means in the English language. I only hope we don't see it creeping into the Press here. I saw it mis-used the other day in the *Daily Express*. But certainly there is much finer writing I think in some sections of the British Press today than there was, say, ten years ago. And long may that process continue. But the trouble is Gresham's Law – the bad tends to drive out the good. And it's much easier to make money by producing shoddy disreputable newspapers than it is by producing very fine papers. I'm very glad to see that Lord Thomson has managed to combine the two – producing excellent papers and making money at the same time.

IRVING: Are you prepared sometimes to admit that the editor must have final responsibility for what appears?

CHURCHILL: Not a signed article.

IRVING: You've battled for a long time over this problem of having your stuff censored.

CHURCHILL: They've got the editorial columns to express their opinions in, and if I've entered into a contract with them to write stuff under my own name it's got to be my stuff, not their stuff. I don't care whether they tear one of my articles to pieces in the editorial columns, say they disagree with what I've said. I don't join a paper because I agree with its political opinions, it's only because I have an opportunity of expressing my own opinions.

IRVING: What's your rhythm of working? Do you find you go in bursts of four or five days' concentrated effort, or do you do a bit every day?

CHURCHILL: Well, I sometimes work much harder than I do at other times. The advantage of working in your own house is that you can work when you like. I do something every day, but often I'm pretty idle for three or four days in a row, then I suddenly get a burst of activity, I get excited about something and then I can work very long hours. But I have no set rules for myself.

IRVING: You do quite a bit of work at night, don't you in fact?

CHURCHILL: Yes, I do. I often feel in the dictating mood after dinner and quite often work till two or two-thirty in the morning.

> The heights by great men reached and kept
> Were not attained by sudden flight
> But they while their companions slept
> Were toiling upward in the night.

There, that's the way I justify my working hours in my own mind.

INDEX

131